Hill birds in north-east Highlands

Field observations over decades - ptarmigan, red grouse, golden plover, dotterel, bird counts

Adam Watson

Publication of this book was aided by the generous sponsorship of Bert McIntosh of Crathes near Banchory in Scotland and McIntosh Plant Hire (Aberdeen) Ltd, Birchmoss, Echt, Westhill, Aberdeenshire AB32 6XL, www.mphltd.co.uk. Published by Paragon Publishing, 4 North Street, Rothersthorpe, Northants, NN7 3JB, UK

First published 2013
© Adam Watson 2013

All rights reserved. No part of this publication may be reproduced, stored in a retrieval system or transmitted in any form or by any means, electronic, mechanical, photocopying, recording or otherwise, without the prior written permission of the copyright owner.

Clachnaben, Crathes, Banchory, Aberdeenshire AB31 5JE, Scotland, UK adamwatson@uwclub.net

ISBN 978-1-78222-101-2

Book design, layout and production management by Into Print
www.intoprint.net +44 (0) 1604 832149

Printed and bound in UK, USA and Australia by Lightning Source

Contents

General introduction	3
1. Hatch-dates of ptarmigan and red grouse, and blaeberry growth and climate	4
2. Darkness on the under-parts of summering golden plover	17
3. Breeding success of golden plover and dotterel, and cranefly abundance	28
4. Abundance of breeding golden plover within and amongst areas	39
5. Decline of breeding golden plover since 1970	64
6. Evidence of no material increase of breeding dotterel in 1940s–90s	80
7. Some counts of birds on moorland and alpine land	91

General introduction

The papers presented below rest on my long-term observations in the course of fieldwork on other projects, chiefly the populations of red grouse and ptarmigan. They were not studies with aims defined at the start. Nonetheless I observed over many years with broadly similar annual effort. The results may therefore be of interest, for published data on these topics by other observers are scanty.

Chapter 1. Hatch-dates of ptarmigan and red grouse, and blaeberry growth and climate

Summary

In 1951–2012, I noted the timing of the first unfolding of blaeberry (*Vaccinium myrtillus*) leaves on alpine land and sub-alpine moorland in north-east Scotland, along with hatch-dates of eggs of ptarmigan (*Lagopus mutus*) on the former and red grouse (*Lagopus lagopus scoticus*) on the latter. On two alpine areas and one sub-alpine area on the Cairnwell hills, where I had the longest runs of data (1964–2012), the mean timing of hatch-dates was unrelated to the calendar year during the run as a whole. This applied also during the first half of the run, in 1964–88. During the second half from 1989–2012, however, it showed negative associations with the year (i.e. earlier as time passed), as expected from the milder climate known to have occurred from data on weather at the nearby village of Braemar. These negative associations were not significant for ptarmigan, but were for red grouse. Mean hatch-dates varied more in 1989–2012 than in 1964–88, though not significantly. Those of ptarmigan on Cairnwell and Meall Odhar and of red grouse on the sub-alpine lower slopes of Cairnwell were correlated positively with the timing of blaeberry growth earlier in the same spring. Hatch-dates of ptarmigan came later than those of red grouse living on the slopes at lower altitude, but were correlated positively with those of red grouse. Mean hatch-dates of both species were not significantly related to April air temperature at Braemar in the first half of the run, but there was a strong negative correlation with April air temperature in 1989–2012 for ptarmigan at Cairnwell and a barely significant one for ptarmigan at Meall Odhar, e.g. earlier in warmer Aprils. For red grouse at Cairnwell, there was a negative association in the later period, but not significant.

Introduction

Chapter 1 in my book *Plants in north-east Highlands* – some studies documented data on the timing of blaeberry growth on alpine land and sub-alpine moorland in upper Deeside south-west of Aberdeen. Here I present hatch-dates of ptarmigan on the former and red grouse on the latter. I tested whether a) hatch-dates showed any trends as the years progressed, b) became more variable in recent decades, c) were related in the two bird species, and d) were related to the timing of blaeberry growth as well as to spring air temperature and snow-lie.

Blaeberry shoots form a material proportion of the spring diet of ptarmigan (Watson 1964) and red grouse. Preliminary observations on Derry Cairngorm in the Cairngorms massif suggested that the breeding success of ptarmigan was associated positively with the timing of blaeberry growth (Watson 1965). Analysis of a longer run of data there confirmed this (Watson *et al.* 1998). A more detailed study at the Cairnwell in the Mounth massif showed the importance of maternal nutrition in spring for the subsequent breeding success of ptarmigan, and of fresh growth of blaeberry as a boost to increased nutritive value for that maternal

Ptarmigan on eggs, Meall Odhar, (AW senior)

Field observations over decades

nutrition (Moss & Watson 1984). In the present paper I compare the timing of blaeberry growth with hatch dates and breeding success of ptarmigan on Derry Cairngorm and also on the Cairnwell and nearby Meall Odhar, and of red grouse on sub-alpine moorland on the lower slopes of the Cairnwell. For the sake of brevity and clarity below, the two Cairnwell areas are called Cairnwell high and Cairnwell low.

Study areas

These were on the hill Derry Cairngorm in the Cairngorms massif north-west of Braemar village, and on the hills of the Cairnwell and Meall Odhar in the Mounth massif 15 km south of Braemar. Braemar is in a valley 90 km south-west of Aberdeen. Study areas have been described elsewhere, with maps showing locations (Watson 1965, 1979; Watson *et al.* 1998). Altitudes at Derry Cairngorm spanned 840–1150 m, Cairnwell high and Meall Odhar 760–939 m, and sub-alpine moorland on low Cairnwell 650–760 m.

Methods

Blaeberry growth

This section is copied from Chapter 1 of my book that is mentioned in the first sentence of the Introduction above. During winter, blaeberry on alpine land is a leafless dwarf woody shrub with greyish green stalks that bear small buds. In spring the buds swell and turn a lighter yellowish green, shortly to become leafy new growth. The date when buds showed the first unfolding of leaves was noted, a conspicuous event when seen on close inspection.

Other species would be suitable. For instance, ling heather (*Calluna vulgaris*) shows a pink spot at the tip of each newly growing shoot-tip, and crowberry (*Empetrum hermaphroditum*) a white spot in the centre of the uppermost whorl of leaves on the shoot-tip. I chose blaeberry, because on alpine land it is leafless in winter, so any new unfolding leaf is more conspicuous and hence less easily overlooked than on heather or crowberry. Growth in crowberry starts marginally earlier than in the other two species, up to a week but usually just a day or two.

I recorded timing as the number of weeks after 20 April, to the nearest week, occasionally to the nearest half-week if there were enough visits to justify this or when growth began within a day or two over a big span of altitude. I chose 20 April at the start of the study, before the more recent changes when springs tended to be milder and growth occasionally began before 20 April. In such cases of growth starting before 20 April, I continued to use the number of weeks, but inserted a minus value. Timing varied within an area, usually some days later at the top than at the foot, and it varied with aspect. Heavy browsing by domestic sheep, red deer (*Cervus elaphus*), mountain hare (*Lepus timidus*), ptarmigan and red grouse delayed the onset, because browsed shoots had to form new tips and leaf buds before growth could start. Browning during cold dry weather in winter and spring killed many shoots, delaying growth in affected plants.

Where soil under shallow snow had not frozen, heat from the ground melted the underside of the snow, creating an airspace, and buds there often showed the first signs of swelling, but did not reach the stage of the first leaf starting to unfold. Prolonged fresh snow and hard frost delayed growth. So did a greater depth of snow remaining

Hen ptarmigan on nest, Derry Cairngorm, May

in spring from a snowy winter, because warm air could not reach plants until the snow had gone.

The record was therefore an average for a study area. In a few years when very warm weather came to all altitudes simultaneously, timing was the same at all altitudes (Watson 1965). More usually there was a delay with altitude, sometimes several weeks.

Mean monthly temperatures came from the climatological station at 339 m altitude (327 m since June 2005) at Braemar village (Meteorological Office (MO) Monthly Weather Report and MO later data), as did the number of mornings with snow lying there (defined as snow covering at least half of the ground) from September to May, and the number of days with air frost from October to April. I described blaeberry plants, their growth in spring, methods of recording the timing of the onset of growth, and the Braemar climatological station.

Hatch dates

Hatch-dates were based on estimated ages of broods, checked by noting hatch-dates of eggs at some nests seen earlier. I recorded the age of each brood to the nearest half-week, and then converted this to days after 31 March. Methods for estimating ages have been described in detail and validated elsewhere (Jenkins *et al*. 1963; Watson 1965; Parr 1975; Watson & Miller 1976).

For the present chapter, I excluded obvious repeat clutches. These occurred only in some years and areas, and came weeks later than the main set of clutches on the same area in the same year. Most were known to have followed desertions of first clutches during snowstorms and the subsequent appearance of pairs showing behaviour typical of the weeks before egg-laying and incubation. A few followed robbing of first clutches by predators.

Results

Mean hatch-dates in relation to calendar year

Figs. 1 to 3 show the time series of data, and Table 1 the hatch-dates and other statistics. I used means for analysis; medians for each area were within one or two days of means. In the entire 1964–2012 run as a whole, correlation coefficients were negative but far from significant at Cairnwell high and low, and at Meall Odhar.

When data were split for each half of the run, coefficients remained not significant in the first half of the run (Table 2). However, all shifted between the first and second halves, towards larger values and negative signs. Nevertheless, the only significant correlation was at Cairnwell low.

Variability of mean hatch-dates amongst years

During the second half of the run, in 1988–2012, the mean hatch-date on both the ptarmigan areas was slightly earlier than during the first half, but only by a day or less. On the Cairnwell low area used by red grouse it came later but by less than a day (Table 1). These differences were small and tests of the differences in mean hatch dates between the first and second halves of the run proved far from significant (T tests in Table 3).

The variances for hatch-dates during the second half exceeded those in the first half (Table 1). Timing became more variable in the second half, and a commonly used index of dispersion confirmed this. A

Eggs in same ptarmigan nest, Derry Cairngorm, May

test for the equality of variances revealed unequal variances in all three cases (Table 3). This gave some evidence against the null hypothesis of no differences in the variances of timing, and for the working hypothesis that assumes greater variability during the second half of the run in recent years.

Timing of blaeberry growth compared with hatching of ptarmigan and red grouse

On the lower slopes occupied by red grouse, plant growth and the hatching of the grouse tended to be earlier than at higher altitudes on ptarmigan ground further up the slope. The timing of blaeberry growth on the Cairnwell high was associated positively with the mean hatch-dates of ptarmigan there and at Meall Odhar, but not significantly (Table 4). In contrast, the timing of blaeberry growth on the Cairnwell low area was correlated positively and significantly with hatch-dates of red grouse there.

Mean hatch-dates of red grouse on the Cairnwell low were correlated positively and significantly with those of ptarmigan on the Cairnwell high area (Table 4). Hatch-dates of ptarmigan on the Cairnwell high and on Meall Odhar were strongly correlated positively, as expected from their very similar altitude and similar snow-lie.

Hatch-dates of ptarmigan on the Cairnwell high were not related to those at Derry Cairngorm, as noted by Watson *et al.* (1998) from a shorter run of data. Most of the study area at Derry Cairngorm stood at much higher altitudes than Cairnwell high, and held more extensive winter snow, which often delayed plant growth for weeks. Also, because of its more northerly location, Derry Cairngorm received much more frequent and heavier snowfalls than the Cairnwell high during late April–June, a season when most of the fresh snowfalls come with northerly winds.

Timing in ptarmigan and red grouse compared with air temperature and snow-lie

The mean timing of hatching in ptarmigan on the Cairnwell and Meall Odhar was associated negatively with April temperature, not significantly in 1964–88, but in 1989–12 strongly so at Cairnwell high and Meall Odhar (Table 5). In the case of red grouse on Cairnwell low, the mean timing of hatching in the first half of the run was associated positively but only weakly with April temperature, but in 1989–12 showed a negative significant correlation with April temperature. On all three areas, the timing of hatching was only poorly associated with the number of mornings with snow lying at Braemar 15 km to the north. However, at Derry Cairngorm the mean hatch-date of ptarmigan was strongly correlated with the number of mornings with snow lying in March at the nearby Derry Lodge, only 1 km from the south-east corner of the study area.

Discussion
Timing in relation to warmer climate

Because of milder climate in the last two decades, an earlier response by hatch-dates of ptarmigan and red grouse might be expected. In fact, the mean hatch-dates differed hardly at all between 1964–88 and 1989–2012. The data indicate greater variability in the later period than in 1964–88.

Mean hatch-dates of both species at the Cairnwell and of ptarmigan at Meall Odhar in 1964–12 were associated with mean April temperature at Braemar village, significantly at Cairnwell high and Meall Odhar, and at Cairnwell low. Correlation coefficients were negative, thus signifying earlier hatching after warm Aprils.

Possible factors confounding expected impacts of warmer climate

A consequence of less snow-lie in winter and spring is that blaeberry and other heath species are exposed more often to the elements and suffer more death of shoots from winter browning, a form of desiccation of plant tissue (Watson *et al.* 1966). This delays the onset of growth in affected shoots, irrespective of warm weather. Also it reduces the food supply for ptarmigan and red grouse.

The flowering shoots of harestail cottongrass (*Eriophorum vaginatum*) appear earlier in spring than most plants, have long been known to be highly nutritious, and are eagerly selected by red deer, mountain hares, ptarmigan and red grouse. In recent years of high deer densities, almost all flowering shoots on both the Cairnwell areas and on Meall Odhar have been eaten by deer herds that concentrated night and day on the peaty ground where these plants abounded (A. Watson, unpublished data). The area is part of a larger region where excessive increases in deer densities have been a chronic problem since 1990 (Staines 1996; Deer Commission for Scotland 1997). The DCS enforced large-scale culling during 2006–11 in an attempt to reduce deer densities, and thus restrict damage to vegetation of national and international importance for conservation.

The heavier grazing left fewer flowering shoots of cotton grass for ptarmigan and red grouse than were available in the 1960s–70s. Also, heavier grazing by deer since 1990 has removed more shoots of blaeberry and other heath species, in turn delaying fresh growth. For both reasons, a consequence of heavier grazing has been less high-quality food available to ptarmigan and red grouse in spring. This would be expected to delay the spring boost to the hens' nutrition, and so delay their egg-laying and the hatch-dates of the eggs (Moss & Watson 1984).

An additional factor is the fickle climate at these altitudes. As Moss & Watson (1984) found, an early onset to growth can be followed by colder weather that prevents further growth and also reduces the nutritive value of the fresh growth that has already occurred. Spring 2012 was an extreme example of this, with the earliest growth that I recorded on Cairnwell high and low areas since 1964. On 27 March the afternoon temperature in the car park at the Cairnwell reached 22C and the previous daily mean maximum temperature for Scotland was broken by a recorded maximum of 23.7C at Aboyne in mid Deeside On that afternoon I found harestail cotton grass flowering shoots, and swollen buds of blaeberry, crowberry and heather at all altitudes on all three study areas. A few days later, snow fell and the mean temperature for April was the coldest recorded at Braemar since 1986. May and June were also unusually cold, May the coldest since 1995, June the coldest since 1991. As a result, plant growth ceased by the end of March, the small amount of it vanished quickly by grazing, and no fresh growth occurred on Cairnwell high area until late May. The ptarmigan and red grouse, which I expected in late March to nest extremely early, in fact nested unusually late, the ptarmigan at Cairnwell high and Meall Odhar especially so, the latest recorded there since the study began in 1964. The sole ptarmigan nest found by Stuart Rae on Cairnwell high contained only 4 eggs, an unusually small clutch, and breeding success was very poor. By contrast, in 2011 I recorded the second earliest timing of growth for the entire study, at the start of April. April 2011 was unusually warm, both species nested early, and their breeding success was unusually productive, with 11 young per hen on Cairnwell high, the best I had ever seen on any area in Scotland.

The value of long-term study is well illustrated by inspecting the data up to 2010 and excluding the last two years, which one can now see were both unusual and extreme. At the end of 2010, analyses showed a broadly similar picture to analyses at the end of 2012, for Tables 1, 2, 3 and 5. However, Table 4 up to 2010 showed a quite different result from Table 4 below (including data for 2011 and 2012). The correlations between the timing of blaeberry growth on Cairnwell high and mean hatch date of ptarmigan on Cairnwell high and on Meall Odhar were positive and significant ($r = 0.636$ and 0.573 respectively on the two areas, $P = 0.0001$ and <0.0001). So was the correlation between hatch dates of ptarmigan on Cairnwell high and red grouse on Cairnwell low ($r = 0.467$, $P = 0.0011$). Had the study not continued up to 2012 inclusive, the disappearance of these three strong correlations would have remained unknown. Obviously, extreme changes in weather as in the last two years, especially in 2012 with extreme warmth in late March followed by a long cold spring, were sufficient to disrupt the earlier simple neat picture.

References

Deer Commission for Scotland (1997). 1996–97 report. The Stationery Office, Edinburgh.

Jenkins, D., Watson, A. & Miller, G.R. (1963). Population studies on red grouse, *Lagopus lagopus scoticus* (Lath.) in north-east Scotland. Journal of Animal Ecology 32, 317–376.

Moss, R. & Watson, A. (1984). Maternal nutrition, egg quality and breeding success of Scottish Ptarmigan *Lagopus mutus*. Ibis 126, 212–220.

Parr, R. (1975) Aging red grouse chicks by primary molt and development. Journal of Wildlife Management 39, 180–190

Staines, B.W. (1996). Red deer. In: The Cairngorms assets (Ed. By N.G. Bayfield & J.W.H. Conroy), 269–283. The Cairngorms Partnership, Grantown-on-Spey, Moray.

Watson, A. (1965). A population study of ptarmigan (*Lagopus mutus*) in Scotland. Journal of Animal Ecology 34, 135–172.

Watson, A. (1979). Bird and mammal numbers in relation to human impact at ski lifts on Scottish hills. Journal of Applied Ecology 16, 753–764.

Watson, A. & Miller, G.R. (1976). Grouse management. Game Conservancy, Fordingbridge.

Watson, A., Miller, G.R. & Green, F.H.W. (1966). Winter browning in heather (*Calluna vulgaris*) and other moorland plants. Transactions of the Botanical Society of Edinburgh 40, 195-203.

Watson, A., Moss, R. & Rae, S. (1998). Population dynamics of Scottish rock ptarmigan cycles. Ecology 79, 1174–1192.

Fig. 1. Mean hatch dates of ptarmigan on study area at Cairnwell high area (days after 31 March). No birds in 2002.

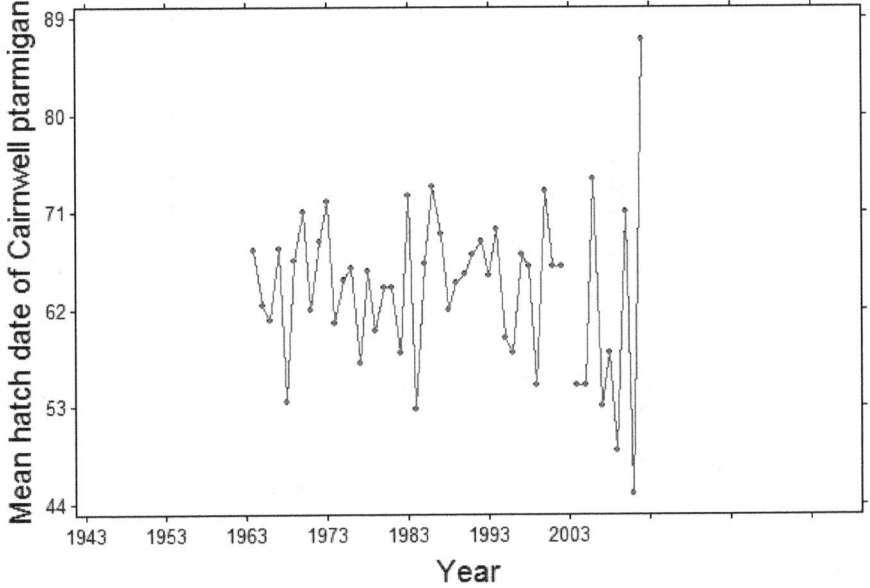

Fig. 2. Mean hatch date Meall Odhar ptarmigan on study area at Meall Odhar (days after 31 March). No birds in 2011.

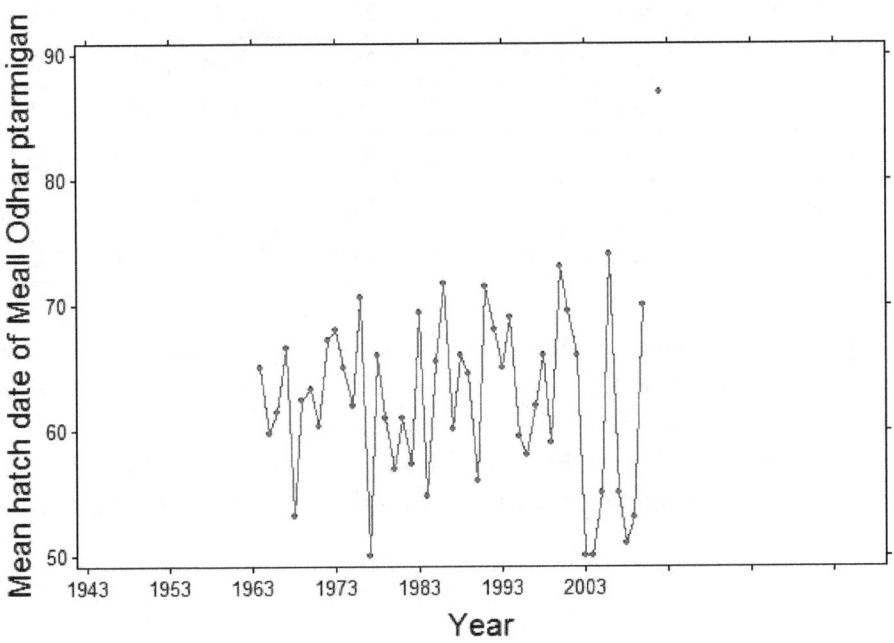

Fig. 3. Mean hatch dates of red grouse on study area at Cairnwell low area (days after 31 March).

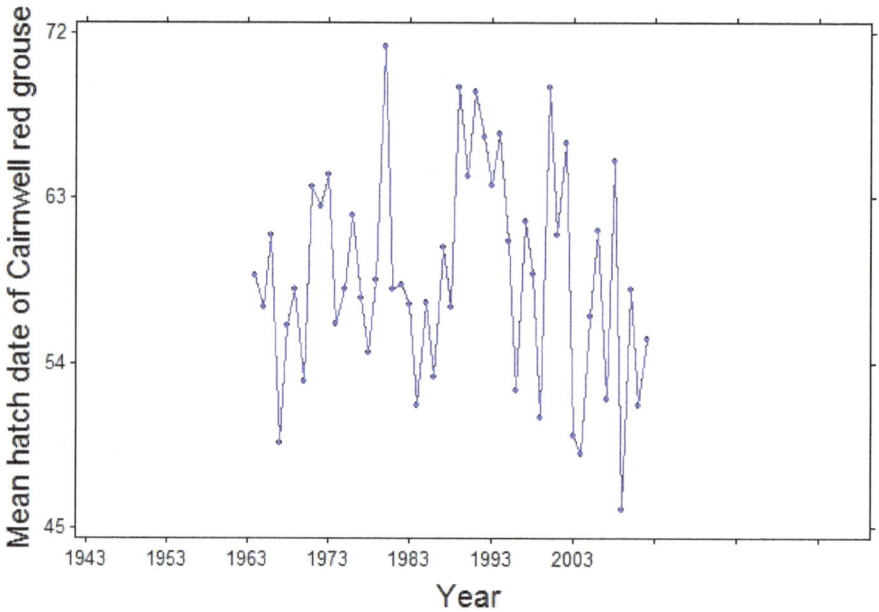

Table 1. Yearly hatch-dates, with mean, variance, index of dispersion (variance divided by mean), and minimum and maximum (days after 31 March).

	Study area	Years	n	Mean	Variance	Index	Min	Max
Ptarmigan	Derry Cairngorm	1951–72	22	76.8	76.6	1.00	60.5	89.7
	Cairnwell high	1964–88	25	64.3	30.2	0.47	52.7	73.3
		1989–12	23	63.3	85.1	1.34	45.0	87.0
	Meall Odhar	1964–88	25	62.6	29.1	0.47	50.0	71.7
		1989–12	23	63.1	84.5	1.34	50.0	87.0
Red grouse	Cairnwell low	1964–88	25	58.2	19.9	0.34	49.5	71.2
		1989–12	24	59.3	49.4	0.83	46.0	69.0

Extreme timings for hatch-dates of individual ptarmigan broods across all years at Derry Cairngorm were 22 May and 30 June, at Cairnwell high on 17 May and 26 June, at Meall Odhar 17 May and 26 June, and for red grouse at Cairnwell low on 15 May and 18 June. The number of years at Cairnwell high and Meall Odhar in 1988–12 was 23, not 24, because no birds occurred in one year at each area (not the same year for both areas).

Table 2. Mean hatch-dates in relation to calendar year.

Timing	Study area	Years	r	P
Ptarmigan	Derry Cairngorm	1951–72	–0.331	0.13
	Cairnwell high	1964–88	0.04	0.86
		1989–12	–0.14	0.52
	Meall Odhar	1964–88	0.07	0.75
		1989–12	–0.008	0.97
Red grouse	Cairnwell low	1964–88	–0.018	0.93
		1989–12	–0.591	0.0024

During the entire run in 1964–2012, correlation coefficients were very low at Cairnwell high, Meall Odhar and Cairnwell low ($n = 48, r = -0.090, -0.042$ and -0.087 respectively, $P = 0.24, 0.78$, and $0.55, n = 48, 48, 49$).

Table 3. Mean timing of hatch-dates compared in 1964–87 and 1988–2012.

	Study area	T	P	F*	P*
Ptarmigan	Cairnwell high	0.43	0.7	2.82	0.0076
	Meall Odhar	0.24	0.8	2.91	0.0063
Red grouse	Cairnwell low	0.67	0.5	2.48	0.0156

* F test for equality of variances, and probability, where $P < 0.05$ gives statistically significant support for assuming unequal variances in early as compared with later year-sets.

Table 4. Timing of blaeberry growth in relation to mean hatch-dates of ptarmigan and red grouse, and timing of blaeberry (and hatch-dates) on one area in relation to another, $n = 21$ at Derry Cairngorm).

Comparison	Study area	r	P
Blaeberry and ptarmigan	Derry Cairngorm	0.519	0.0048
	Cairnwell high	0.255	0.08
	Meall Odhar*	0.201	0.17
Blaeberry and red grouse	Cairnwell low	0.441	0.0015
Blaeberry	Derry Cairngorm and the Cairnwell	−0.140	0.7
Ptarmigan and red grouse	Cairnwell high and low	0.395	0.0054
Ptarmigan	The Cairnwell and Meall Odhar	0.876	<0.0001

* Blaeberry timing recorded on the nearby Cairnwell high area 1 km away.

Table 5. Mean hatch-dates of ptarmigan and red grouse on the Cairnwell and Meall Odhar in relation to mean air temperature at Braemar, and of ptarmigan at Derry Cairngorm in relation to number of March mornings with snow lying at Derry Lodge ($n = 19$ years).

	Study area	Years	r	P
Ptarmigan and April temperature	Cairnwell high	1964–88	−0.311	0.13
		1989–12	−0.677	0.0004
	Meall Odhar	1964–88	−0.203	0.33
		1989–12	−0.562	0.0053
Red grouse and April temperature	Cairnwell low	1964–88	0.275	0.18
		1989–12	−0.597	0.0021
Ptarmigan and snow days Derry Lodge	Derry Cairngorm	1954–73	0.584	0.009

Chapter 2. Darkness on the under-parts of breeding golden plover

Summary

I assessed the extent of black plumage on the under-parts of breeding golden plover (*Pluvialis apricaria*) on several areas of moorland and alpine land. It varied greatly within each area. Cocks exceeded hens in its extent. I found no evidence for birds at high altitude being darker than at low altitude; if anything, the opposite occurred. This fitted with Parr (1980), who found the darkest population of Scottish breeding cocks so far recorded, on moorland at yet lower altitude. The extent of dark plumage did not differ materially within areas amongst years, even though arrival on territories varied by over two months between mild and wintry springs. Cocks and hens tended to pair with birds resembling them in plumage darkness and not randomly with respect to darkness.

Introduction

In the early 20th century it was generally held that golden plovers breeding in Britain were of a southern subspecies, whereas birds in more northerly countries belonged to a northern subspecies (e.g. Witherby *et al.* 1940). The northern race had more black on the under-parts, with a conspicuous white band between the black and the yellowish upper-parts. Exceptions in southern regions were known, however. For instance Chapman (1889) wrote that the breasts of Northumbrian birds at most were only marbled, whereas those in Shetland and southern Norway

Eggs of a red grouse hatching, Kerloch near Banchory, May 1969

approached much more closely to the plumage of birds breeding in the far north, while birds in Finnmark were 'perfectly black beneath', but in 1921 he sketched a Northumbrian bird with black underparts of northern type (Chapman 1924). Tucker (1949) and other authors cited by Wynne-Edwards (1957) reported other such British exceptions.

Smith (1957) found that flocks in Midlothian during April, mostly at reservoirs, were of northern type, probably migrants from Scandinavia, when local breeding birds were dispersed on territories. Local birds had acquired full summer dress in March, when the flocks at reservoirs still retained the pale underparts of the winter dress. Smith's paper led Wynne-Edwards (1957) to write that many birds on the Aberdeenshire side of the Cairngorms had northern-type plumage.

His review of the literature revealed a great variety from northern to southern types in Britain, Faeroe and Iceland. He wrote that the proportion 'of the more resplendent types undoubtedly increases northwards' but argued that it was unjustified to assign a different subspecies.

His paper led to an approach by the journal (Editors 1957) to several ornithologists with much experience of the Highlands, requesting their views. The group of notes revealed 'that breeding golden plovers which resemble typical "northern-race" birds are much more common in the Highlands than has been generally realised'. Watson (1957) suggested that there might be a cline of variation, with well-marked birds tending to occur more frequently towards the north and possibly towards higher altitudes. He had seen northern-type birds on Deeside

Golden plover and ptarmigan forage in a field before their nesting period, Hrisey, north Iceland, snowy peaks beyond, May 1965

Nest of golden plover, Hill of Wirren near Edzell, May 1980

moors at 400–460 m, and on alpine land in the Cairngorms area. He wrote 'Whether these variants occur as frequently on the lower moors as on the high tops is a problem that could be elucidated only by a lot more field-watching.' Subsequently in 1958 he assessed the plumage of all birds seen on several study areas. The data are the basis for this paper.

When Raymond Parr in the 1970s proposed intensive work on golden plovers at Kerloch moor in lower Deeside, I suggested that he measure the frequency of plumage types. By marking many birds with colour rings, he could follow the plumage of the same individuals and their offspring in different years (Parr 1980). Although plumage variation was not the main aim, his advance in understanding it has not been bettered.

In Norway, Byrkjedal (1978) found that southern coastal breeders had paler under-parts than breeders on alpine land at the same latitude and paler than coastal breeders further north. He argued for two subspecies, suggesting that occasional dark birds in southern areas might be wayward northern birds staying in the south instead of migrating to the far north. Also he referred to writers who speculated that sexually immature birds might be less distinctively coloured, and so pale birds in a predominantly dark population may be immature yearlings. As Parr (1980) pointed out, 'Only the use of marked birds can decide such matters', and his use of them produced results that reject the above speculations about migrants and yearlings. He found that dark birds which were breeding in any one year tended to return next year to breed, and that yearling birds were as dark as older ones, and bred when yearlings.

Byrkjedal & Thompson (1998) reviewed the problem. They stated that the small overlap in darkness between the two coastal populations in south-west Norway and other Norwegian populations 'suggests that the two forms are geographically and morphologically sufficiently well defined to be regarded as valid subspecies', but then add '– but only just'. However, this argument was dubious, because the other coastal populations studied were 200 km or more to the north, and birds on intermediate land were not studied. These authors then stated confusingly that the validity of the two subspecies 'remains to be resolved. However, we agree with the recent literature (e.g. Glutz von Blotzheim *et al.* 1975; Cramp & Simmons 1983) that workers should refrain from the trinomial designation of the Eurasian Golden Plover'. This contradicted the statement of Byrkjedal & Thompson about 'valid subspecies'. The Summary of their Chapter 3, however, added confusion by taking a contradictory tack, 'Presently, there is little evidence for two subspecies of Eurasian Golden Plover'.

In the Summary of Chapter 4, they wrote 'Breeding plumage patterns may be strongly associated with disruptive colouration in contrast-rich habitats (black-white face, breast and belly contrasts), and timing of breeding (less contrasting Eurasian Golden Plovers breed earliest)'. However, their idea about contrast pertained to different individual pairs being on territories with vegetation of different contrast, within populations, whereas the timing of breeding pertained to a different question, involving average differences between populations in widely different regions. Here again their argument was confused.

They wrote 'In areas such as the Cairngorms and Sutherland, Scotland, birds nesting at lower altitudes seem to be paler than those at high altitudes', but adduced no data. Their statement conflicted with and ignored the evidence of Parr (1980), which showed a high proportion of dark types on a Scottish moor at low altitude.

Study areas

These were chosen for research on red grouse (*Lagopus lagopus scoticus*) and ptarmigan (*Lagopus mutus*), and I made observations on golden plovers in the course of work on the other species. Most areas lay in Glen Esk, Angus, and two in upper Deeside, Aberdeenshire. All supported heather moorland, except for alpine land on the Braid Cairn and nearby hills in Glen Esk, and on Beinn a' Bhuird in the Cairngorms. The two areas studied in most detail were the Low and High areas near Tarfside in Glen Esk. All areas have been described elsewhere (Jenkins *et al.* 1963; Jenkins & Watson 2001), except Easter Balloch which was not a defined study area, and Beinn a' Bhuird which was area B described by Watson (1989).

Methods

In April 1958 I devised scores using the four types drawn by Wynne-Edwards (1957), along with three others, a paler type that lacked dark feathering on the face or neck, the next palest with the belly mostly white, and the palest birds with no black on the under-parts. Below, I express these as 1 for palest to 7 for 'northern'. In the field I scored the plumage of all birds seen, pair by pair, and in flock birds foraging in grass fields beside the Low area in Glen Esk.

Newly hatched chicks of golden plover, Carn nan Sac near Cairnwell, May 1971

I assumed that cocks were darker on the under-parts than hens. This assumption rests on museum specimens, marked birds, and behaviour (Witherby *et al.* 1943; Parr 1980; Byrkjedal & Thompson 1998).

When Parr (1980) began a more detailed study at Kerloch, I suggested he use scores and showed him mine. He used 8 grades and Byrkjedal & Thompson (1998) published a drawing by Chris Thomas showing 10. Rae *et al.* (in press) used Thomas's grades. My 4 to 7 therefore resemble Parr's 4 to 7 and the four types illustrated by Wynne-Edwards, and my 4 to 7 resemble Thomas's 6 to 9. My 3 below refers to scores 2 and 3 in Parr and 3 to 5 in Thomas, my 2 denotes Parr's 1 and covers Thomas's 1 and 2, and my 1 is the same as Parr's and Thomas's 0.

Results

There was no evidence that breeding birds in 1958 were darker on the High area than birds on the nearby Low area (Table 1). If anything, those on the High area were slightly paler, especially the hens ($U = 114$, $P = 0.087$).

Because Parr (1980) found a statistically significant tendency for assortative mating in terms of dark plumage, I present the 1958 data from the High and Low areas in the same way (Table 2). Analysis revealed that cocks and hens tended to pair assortatively (3 x 2 table, combining cock grade 7 with 6, and hen grade 5 with 4, because of small sample size, $\chi^2 = 15.64$, $P = 0.0004$).

Beside the Low area, flocks foraged on grass fields during the end of April and in May, when birds on the moor were incubating eggs. Because Parr (1980) found that incubating birds during daylight were usually cocks, whereas hens incubated at night, one might expect birds in the fields to be hens off duty. Birds in flocks tended to be slightly paler than hens that I had seen paired with cocks on the moor, however. One snag was that some hens in flocks may have involved the same individuals as I saw on other days when paired with cocks on the moor, so I have not analysed the differences because of lack of robust statistical independence. Others in the flock may have been waiting to breed sequentially, as Parr (1979) found at Kerloch. The lack of marked birds in my case made it impossible to separate these confounding questions about flock birds.

On Monagob and Corndavon in 1958, birds had plumage scores very similar to those on the High and Low areas in Glen Esk (Table 1). Likewise, birds on alpine land on high hills in Glen Esk and Beinn a' Bhuird appeared similar to those on moorland.

An obvious qualification is that most data for this paper came from only one year, 1958. However, scattered observations in Watson (1957) and others since then were consistent with the 1958 data. During intensive work on red grouse at the Glen Esk areas in 1959–62, I saw no obvious differences from 1958. The spring of 1958 was unusually cold and snowy, but spring in 1961 was unusually mild. In spring 1961 I noted the plumage of paired birds on the High area. The data closely resemble those from the High area in 1958 (Table 1). Moreover, birds could not nest on the plateau of Beinn a' Bhuird in the exceptionally wintry May and early June 1977, because the nesting grounds lay under deep continuous snow, which did not start to decrease in cover until 15 June and showed major clearance only after 18 June. Despite the lateness of nesting, birds showed no obvious difference in dark plumage.

In 1969 and 1983 at Corgarff in Strathdon, I observed flocks in grass fields when deep snow covered the breeding grounds on nearby hills. These flocks included many cocks as well as hens. When viewed in sunlight at close range through binoculars from a car, the faces of the darkest cocks were noted as being 'not yet jet black, but sepia or dark cocoa', and the pale band behind the face as not white but pale creamy.

Discussion

My finding that birds on high moorland at Glen Esk in 1958 had plumage no darker than on low moorland, if anything slightly paler, fits with Parr's (1980) results on the even lower moor of Kerloch. There, breeding cocks had even darker plumage than at Glen Esk. Admittedly these results came from different observers, who did not test their scores on the same birds to check error within or between observers. However, at the start of Parr's study I suggested that he measure plumage and we discussed grades on published sketches by Wynne-Edwards and Chapman, on photographs in Tucker (1949), and in relation to birds that we watched from a vehicle during the first spring of his study. Hence it is unlikely that such a marked difference in darkness of cocks was due to material difference between observers. Interestingly, Parr's data show that his hens were paler than at Glen Esk.

Watson (1966) wrote of golden plovers on alpine land in the Cairngorms in spring, 'Some of them appear to be non-breeders, staying in small groups and not pairing up; these have little or no black on the face,
throat or belly'. For example, two nearby flocks on Glas Maol totalled 31 birds on 30 May 1972, when others were dispersed in pairs and I had found a nest with three eggs on 20 May. Pale birds as in the above quotation would classify as grades 1–2, yet I recorded no paired birds in grades 1–2 on many study areas. Hence it seems likely that these pale birds were non-breeders or perhaps sequential breeders waiting for a vacant territory as proved by Parr with marked birds at Kerloch.

Byrkjedal (1978) suggested that the proportion of black variants is greater in lichen-dominated alpine and arctic areas, while the proportion of paler variants is greater in moors and lowland raised bogs with much sedge and heather. Byrkjedal & Thompson (1998) reported a correlation between the proportion of dark variants on different areas in Norway and a score for 'habitat contrast', where contrast in each pair's territory was ranked in increasing 'contrast-richness' from grass/sedge through heather moor and *Racomitrium* heath to lichen heath.

Such an association of events is not necessarily cause and effect. A possible interpretation is that a dark bird chooses a territory where its plumage resembles that territory's colour. There are other snags with the idea of habitat contrast, such as that sedge mixed with heather has more contrast than either sedge alone or heather alone, and perhaps more than *Racomitrium* heath.

Byrkjedal & Thompson (1998) suggested that the amount of dark plumage in different areas may be fixed between years, in relation to the average date of spring-like conditions, or that it may vary from year to year according to the varying onset of spring. These suggestions were speculative, with no data adduced.

They can be rejected by the evidence of Parr (1980), who found that the same individually marked birds did not change in plumage type between years. Byrkjedal & Thompson argued that because Parr 'did not relate this to spring phenology or the birds' time of arrival, this needs to be examined more carefully'. Their criticism was unwarranted, for Parr presented data showing little inter-year variation in the date of arrival on the fields and the territories, but also showing a correlation between the arrival date and the minimum February air temperature. In any case, given that the range of variation over Parr's seven years was only 18 days for arrival dates in the fields and six days for arrival dates on territories, the idea that this small variation could cause a large variation in darkness between years seems implausible speculation. Also, most birds had already attained the nuptial plumage on arrival and apparently all had done so by early March, although Parr did not publish on this because the point was so obvious. Smith (1957) also found that local birds on territories on the Midlothian moorland were already in nuptial plumage when arriving in late February.

Another speculation in Byrkjedal & Thompson was that the paler plumage of southern breeders may be an 'energetic consequence' of early breeding, such that birds stop moulting early and skip growing the dark plumage, so as to shift energy reserves into breeding. This too seems unlikely. The birds studied by Parr on low moorland in north-east Scotland, a southern area, arrived from winter quarters in late February, many weeks before nesting, and their nuptial plumage was already quite dark. Likewise, northern birds remain in flocks in Scotland until the end of April or early May, and do not turn dark until April or exceptionally late March (Smith 1957).

Furthermore, birds in my study did not differ in the darkness of their under-parts between years (e.g. Table 1). This was despite a more than two-month variation in arrival dates at the High area in Glen Esk (mid February 1961 and the end of April 1958). It was also despite a very late start to nesting on Beinn a' Bhuird plateau until late June 1977 (as on arctic tundra) because of exceptionally wintry conditions.

Darker under-parts in northern than in southern regions occur also in dunlin (*Calidris alpina*) and some other northern wader species, and many passerine species in northern regions are larger and more brightly coloured over the whole body than in the south (Chapman 1924; Witherby *et al.* 1938). When current workers make speculative explanations of specific aspects in golden plovers, it may help understanding if these are set in this wider context.

Parr's (1980) evidence showed statistically significant assortative pairing in relation to darkness or paleness of under-parts in golden plover that were breeding at Kerloch, e.g. dark cocks tended to pair with dark hens. Surprisingly, Byrkjedal & Thompson (1998) did not mention this. The present study provides further evidence confirming Parr on this.

References

Byrkjedal, I. (1978). Variation and secondary intergradation in SW-Norwegian golden plover *Pluvialis apricaria* populations. Ornis Scandinavica 9, 101–110.

Byrkjedal, I. & Thompson, D.B.A. (1998). Tundra plovers. Poyser, London.

Chapman, A. (1889). Bird-life of the Borders. Gurney & Jackson, London.

Chapman, A. (1924). The Borders and beyond. Gurney & Jackson, London.

Editors (1957). Gordon, S., Hewson, R., Nethersole-Thompson, D., Tewnion, A. & Watson, A. (separate notes by each author, preceded by editorial note, Editors A. Watson, V.C. Wynne-Edwards, J.W. Campbell & W.U. Flower. 'Northern' golden plovers in northern parts of Scotland. Scottish Naturalist 69, 120–124.

Jenkins, D., Watson, A. & Miller, G.R. (1963). Population studies on red grouse, Lagopus lagopus scoticus (Lath.) in north-east Scotland. Journal of Animal Ecology 32, 317–376.

Jenkins, D. & Watson, A. (2001). Bird numbers in relation to grazing on a grouse moor from 1957–61 to 1988–98. Bird Study 48, 18–22.

Parr, R. (1979). Sequential breeding by golden plovers. British Birds 72, 499–503.

Parr, R. (1980). Population study of golden plover *Pluvialis apricaria* using marked birds. Ornis Scandinavica 11, 179–189.

Smith, R.W.J. (1957). 'Northern' golden plovers in Midlothian during spring. Scottish Naturalist 69, 84–88.

Tucker, B.W. (1949). A note on racial variation in golden plovers. British Birds 42, 383–384.

Watson, A. (1957). 'Northern' golden plovers in northern parts of Scotland. Scottish Naturalist 69, 123–124.

Watson, A. (1966). Hill birds of the Cairngorms. Scottish Birds 4, 179–203.

Watson, A. (1989). Dotterel populations and spacing on three Scottish areas in 1967–86. Ornis Fennica 66, 85–99.

Witherby, H.F., Jourdain, F.C.R., Ticehurst, N.F. & Tucker, B.W. (1938, 1940). The handbook of British birds. Vols 1 & 2 (1938), and 4 (1943). Witherby, London.

Wynne-Edwards, V.C. (1957). The so-called 'northern golden plover'. Scottish Naturalist 69, 89–93.

Table 1. Proportion (%) of paired birds with different plumage types to fit those of Parr (1980), on High and Low and Monagob areas at Glen Esk and on upper Deeside in late April–early June 1958, and on the High area at Glen Esk in 1961. Data cover all paired birds seen on these areas during total counts of red grouse and other birds.

		n	3	4	5	6	7	Mean
Cock	High	13	0	31	38	31	0	5.00
	Low	25	0	16	60	20	4	5.12
	Monagob	6	0	17	50	33	0	4.83
	Corndavon	8	0	13	63	25	0	5.17
	Glen Esk alpine*	10	0	30	40	30	0	5.00
	Beinn a' Bhuird	6	0	17	50	33	0	5.17
	High, 1961	12	0	25	42	33	0	5.08
Hen	High	13	77	23	0	0	0	3.23
	Low	25	48	48	4	0	0	3.56
	Monagob	6	67	33	0	0	0	3.33
	Corndavon	8	63	37	0	0	0	3.37
	Glen Esk alpine*	10	60	40	0	0	0	3.40
	Beinn a' Bhuird^	6	67	33	0	0	0	3.33
	High, 1961	12	42	50	8	0	0	3.67

Areas where golden plover were seen on Low and High areas in Glen Esk were at 220–350 m altitude and 500–655 m respectively, Monagob at 270–360 m on Gannochy in lower Glen Esk, and Corndavon at 410–500 m in upper Deeside.

* In Glen Esk, at 760–890 m on the east slope of the Braid Cairn (two pairs), combined with eight pairs at 760–830 m on the upper parts of Easter Balloch and Wester Balloch.

^ Alpine plateau at 900–1200 m north of Braemar in upper Deeside.

In a total of 33 seen during May in flocks on fields beside the Low area, one bird was scored 1, 11 score 2, 11 score 3, 7 had score 4, and 3 birds had score 5, with a mean of 3.0. I did no statistical analysis of these grades in relation to those in the Table, because some birds seen in the fields may have been the same individuals as those seen on other occasions at the Low or nearby High area.

During daily observations in the cold snowy spring of 1958, the first bird on territory was seen at the Low area on 24 April, the first at the High area on 25 April. On 3–5 May I saw many on territories at the Low area, but none at the High area, though all had returned to the latter on 7 May. By contrast, in the very mild spring of 1961, birds had dispersed on territory and were singing on 16 February at the Low area and on 18–19 February at the High area. This big difference of more than two months between years was not reflected in any material difference in darkness of birds.

Table 2. The number of cocks with scores 4, 5, 6 or 7 that were paired with hens of score 3 or 4 on the Low and High areas in late April–early June 1958. Pairings of cock or hen with birds of other scores were not seen.

		Cock 4	Cock 5	Cock 6	Cock 7
High	Hen 3	4	5	1	0
	Hen 4	0	0	3	0
Low	Hen 3	4	8	0	0
	Hen 4	0	7	5	0
	Hen 5	0	0	0	1
High + Low	Hen 3	8	13	1	0
	Hen 4	0	7	8	0
	Hen 5	0	0	0	1

Chapter 3. Breeding success of golden plover and dotterel, and cranefly abundance

Summary

Breeding success (the number of young reared per adult), was noted in golden plover (*Pluvialis apricaria*) and dotterel (*Charadrius morinellus*) on Glas Maol in the east Mounth hill-range in north-east Scotland. In both species it was positively correlated with a score for the abundance of adult craneflies, mostly *Tipula montana*, one of the main foods of adult birds and chicks. Craneflies abounded every second year. On Cairn Gorm plateau, dotterel occurred each year, golden plover only in some years. Breeding success of dotterel at Cairn Gorm was associated positively with the cranefly score but insignificantly. I attribute this difference from Glas Maol to more frequent summer snowfalls at the higher more northerly Cairn Gorm, a random weather factor associated with poor breeding success.

Introduction

In this paper I present a long run of data on breeding success of golden plover and dotterel on Glas Maol, an alpine hill in Scotland, in relation to the abundance of one of their main foods, craneflies.

Much study has been done in the last few decades on breeding success of dotterel, but relatively little on golden plover. Most golden plover in Britain breed on moorland, and it is hard to see chicks because they hide under vegetation. Although one can infer from the adults' behaviour that they have young, often the chicks remain unseen. Trained dogs find them readily by scent and sight, especially when chicks are close together soon after leaving the nest, but dogs can easily miss scattered chicks. The only time when all chicks in a brood can be readily found on moorland is when they are large and beginning to fly, or almost fully grown and able to fly. Because alpine vegetation is prostrate, chicks can seldom hide under it, and so dogs and observers can find them more easily than on moorland. On alpine land it is also easier to see craneflies, one of the main foods of golden plover and dotterel there, because they are conspicuous on the short vegetation and on bare ground.

Cranefly adults and larvae form a high proportion of the diet of dotterel in years of major cranefly emergence (Galbraith *et al.* 1996), and adult golden plover and chicks can be seen to take adult and larval craneflies amongst vegetation and on the ground. Byrkjedal (1980) found that about half of the diet of adult golden plover on alpine land in south Norway during May consisted of larval craneflies. Hence it is useful to compare the numbers and breeding success of golden plover and dotterel with the abundance of craneflies, and I do this below for two alpine areas.

Study areas

Most work was on area C (see Watson 1988, 1989 for detail). The area covered 107 ha of Glas Maol plateau, rising from 950 m to the summit at 1068 m. Area C of a later intensive study (Galbraith *et al.* 1993; Thompson & Whitfield 1993) included it, but also much ground outside, in total 270 ha (Thompson *et al.* 2003).

The bedrock of Dalradian schist supported a relatively thick base-rich topsoil, supporting a vegetation cover with little or no bare ground except on exposed ridges and scattered boulders.

I also used area A of Watson (1988, 1989) on Cairn Gorm plateau, covering 1187 ha at 1000–1300 m. Area A of a later more intensive study by other workers covered 778 ha of it, later cut to 457 ha (Holt & Whitfield 1996a). Confusingly, Thompson & Whitfield (1993) used the terms 'study area' and 'site' as A for Drumochter and B for Cairn Gorm, whereas Thompson *et al.* (2003) again used 'study areas' and 'sites' but B for Cairn Gorm and A for Drumochter.

Both sections of A lay on granite bedrock, with thinner and more acidic topsoil than at the same altitude and aspect on Glas Maol. There occurred a higher proportion of bare ground, mostly consisting of coarse granite granules and boulder fields. Per unit area, the number and size of snow patches in summer exceeded those on any other Scottish hill at the same altitude.

No golden plover summered in most years on A, where they were scarce and found only on a 260-ha central section, whereas at Glas Maol they occurred every summer. Dotterel bred annually on both areas.

Methods
Birds
On Glas Maol during spring, golden plover arrived in flocks, which later dispersed as pairs on territories as the weather warmed, snow melted, and ground thawed. The pairs were located by scanning with binoculars, and were easy to find on the pale short arctic-alpine vegetation because of their large size and dark colour. I tried to move on without disturbing or flushing the birds, so as to avoid the risk of counting the same birds more than once. Also, each bird and each pair differed in the amount of black on the under-parts, and sketches of this allowed me to distinguish all birds seen within each count, and indeed to achieve a total enumeration of birds present, as in counts of Scottish ptarmigan in spring (Watson 1965).

Though golden plover are cryptic when sitting on nests or downy chicks, a person approaching a brood induces frequent loud calling and diversionary displays by parents, especially if one has a dog.

At the dusk and dawn chorus, cock golden plover sing loudly on and above their territories and can be located at >1 km in calm air or a light wind, using methods described for red grouse (Watson & O'Hare 1979a). The number of cocks heard during dusk and dawn watches on blanket bog in Co Mayo agreed very closely with the number of pairs seen during counts on the same areas in daylight using pointing dogs (Watson & O'Hare 1979b). The dogs had been trained to search areas during counts of red grouse or ptarmigan, and to point at other animals such as golden plover and dotterel.

When Raymond Parr made an intensive study of golden plover at Kerloch moor and later he added a study of wading birds on blanket bog in relation to dense planting of coniferous trees in Caithness, he had years of experience of using pointing dogs for counts of red grouse, as well as of scanning for red grouse and other moorland birds and mammals with binoculars during slow transect walks. I suggested that for the detailed study of golden plover and other waders he should also make observations at dawn and dusk, as at Glenamoy, and he did. At Kerloch, he (1990a) achieved a near-total enumeration of golden plover, using marked birds in an intensive study that relied on counts with pointing dogs and scanning on foot and from vehicles, as well as prolonged watches from vehicles used as mobile hides.

Checks by Parr (1990b, 1992a) on Kerloch and on blanket bog in Caithness showed that the number of singing golden plover and red grouse (and in Caithness also dunlin) during dusk and dawn watches agreed closely with the number of pairs seen by the other methods (see especially Appendix B of Parr 1990b, and also Parr 1992a). Hence it is reasonable to infer that counts with dogs and scanning by walking in transects without dogs result in a near-total enumeration of golden plover and dunlin. Adding confidence to this is that he and I did dusk and dawn watches at 10 study areas in Caithness, on each occasion combining with the two of us on a given area, standing on different vantage points far apart and out of sight and hearing of one another. The results (see Appendix C of Parr 1990b, and also Parr 1992b) showed almost total agreement between us for the number of singing golden plover, dunlin, red grouse, greenshank, curlew and snipe.

I assessed the breeding success of golden plover by the above same scanning method as in spring, noting the number of big young and adults before the young had become fully grown and independent. Big young were well feathered and able to fly short distances, but still retained down on the head and neck, and wisps of down on the back. Chicks in their last week of growth could be told from adults by their uniformly yellowish-gold upper parts compared with the more patchy appearance of moulting adults, their complete lack of any black on the under parts, and traces of white down immediately above the bill and on the nape. The traces of down were conspicuous in sunlight, especially when viewed against the light, when they appeared silvery. Even when young had become full grown and independent, lacking any traces of down, the above uniform plumage characters were still conspicuous and diagnostic.

Counts of young and old golden plover were done between mid June and mid July. One visit in late summer was usually insufficient, because some birds failed with first nests. Either they or birds replacing them then displayed before a repeat late nest. In some such cases, eggs had not hatched by the time that first broods had become independent. For instance, a pair at Glas Maol had chicks only a few days old on 1 August 1982. If it were obvious that any birds had re-nested after failure, I made another visit to check broods between late July and mid August. Count dates varied between years, according to the timing of breeding each year, which I knew from observations of snow cover and plover behaviour during spring visits.

Other snags were that golden plover were often wilder than dotterel, and it took longer to tell fully-grown young from old because their plumage differences were less conspicuous than those with dotterel. In consequence, in some years only a sample of the golden plover present could be differentiated into young and old, whereas I could differentiate all dotterel present.

I studied the numbers and breeding success of dotterel by methods described

Low study area near Tarfside, Glen Esk, September 1957

elsewhere (Watson & Rae 1987; Watson 1988, 1989). By 'numbers' I meant the number of adults in May, once pairs had settled and were being seen repeatedly in the same locations. By breeding success I meant the number of big young seen in late July or early August, divided by the number of settled cocks in spring.

At Glas Maol, Watson (1988, 1989) gave data on numbers and breeding success up to 1986 inclusive. Also there are data from fieldwork on numbers and breeding success by Robert Rae and me for 1987 (unpublished), on breeding success for 1988–91 in Thompson & Whitfield (1993), and on numbers and breeding success for 1988–94 in Holt & Whitfield (1996b). Also I made observations in 1988–94 and several later years

On numbers, it should be noted that Thompson & Whitfield for Glas Maol stated 'No data' for various bird species in 1987, although I had counts of several species in that spring. Their sole exception involved dotterel, where they gave 19 as the number of breeding attempts, their surrogate measure of numbers. They warned that the number of breeding attempts will exceed the number of cocks, because some relay after failure of the first nest. The value 19 for 1987 was 'Estimated principally from work by A. Watson and R. Rae'. It greatly surpassed that in all other years of their study, when the number of annual attempts varied from 9 to 13. I regard their 19 estimate as too high for other reasons. Broods move from day to day. Hence, inconsistency between counts increases the smaller the study area, simply because the length of the boundary relative to the surface area also rises. Glas Maol was the smallest area for me and for later workers.

The likelihood of seeing new broods not seen earlier also rises disproportionately for the same reason. An estimate is inflated further if many observations are late in the season, as in 1987. Broods tend to move further then and often concentrate in loose groups on the upper parts of a given area.

For numbers at Cairn Gorm, Watson (1988, 1989) gave data up to 1986 inclusive, and Holt & Whitfield (1996a) for 1987–94. Data on breeding success at Cairn Gorm are in Thompson & Whitfield (1993) from 1987–91, and in Holt & Whitfield (1996a) from 1987–93. Also I made observations in several years after 1986.

For 1988–90 inclusive, I do not use data on breeding success at Glas Maol from Thompson & Whitfield or my own observations, because poor field-craft by two inexperienced observers in these three summers led to abnormally high rates of nest desertion and nest predation, and also a low return rate by adults in the next spring, in short, unnatural invalid data.

Craneflies
To assess the abundance of adult craneflies, I made visual estimates annually during the period from mid June to mid July (but on Cairn Gorm did not make notes on this in 1982–95, as reported by Watson (1997)). Vegetation was so short that craneflies could not easily hide, and tended to run or fly off as one walked near them. I scored the abundance of adult craneflies in five categories 1–5, from 1 for scarce, through 4 for numerous, to 5 very abundant. In years of category 1, I would see none on the area on some days, and very few on others. Probably I would have seen more if I had concentrated my fieldwork on craneflies,

but this was not so, and my effort each year was broadly the same.

I saw one case of category 5 in July 1977 on Glas Maol, described in Watson (1996) as huge numbers, up to 20 per m², their wings rustling as they flew off. Another case there was in June 2009. The scores are effectively on an approximately logarithmic scale, with score 1 equivalent to about 1 cranefly seen per day, score 2 to about 10, 3 to 100, 4 to 1000, and score 5 to 10000 or more craneflies.

In some years at Cairn Gorm their abundance was not uniform across the whole area. For example, in 1972 and 1976, which were not peak years for craneflies on the entire study area, their emergence on the central part was almost as large as in the general peak years of 1973 and 1977. Other observations on this at Cairn Gorm are in an internal unpublished report (Holt & Whitfield 1996a). Only in 1988 did I find them abundant on one part of Glas Maol in a summer when they were scarce on the study area as a whole. This was on a ridge outside though close to the study area, covering only 50 ha and too steep for nesting golden plover or dotterel.

Watson (1997) observed that snow patches delay the emergence, which shows a localised spring-like peak as snow-free ground thaws and warms, continuing into August. Because the plateau south of Cairn Gorm is the snowiest place in Scotland during summer, this helps explain the less synchronised emergence. Other differences are the greater range of altitude at Cairn Gorm and the wider variety of habitat (Watson 1981).

In 1994–96 the annual emergence of craneflies (mostly *Tipula montana*) on the upper parts of Glas Maol was highly

Corndavon study area near Crathie, October 1985

synchronised within years (Smith 1997). Peak abundance within any one year came in a period lasting only 7–10 days, usually in the last week of June–early July, but varying by up to two weeks between years. The life cycle takes two years at high altitudes, with flies emerging in their second year, as found by Hofsvang (1972) studying the closely related T. excisa in Norway, and Smith (1997) on Glas Maol. A strongly biennial pattern of emergence occurs, with high numbers of adults every second year. This was also the case in Smith's study, with a peak in 1995 and lows in 1994 and 1996, and his estimates of numbers showed approximately a tenfold difference between successive years. The biennial pattern with peaks in odd-numbered years also occurred at Cairn Gorm (Watson 1997). However, peaks in even-numbered years have been found at Drumochter in the central Highlands (Galbraith et al. 1996).

To conclude, the main issues were that the abundance alternated in a biennial pattern on both Cairn Gorm and Glas Maol, with high numbers in odd-numbered years and scarcity in even-numbered ones, and that abundance differed greatly from year to year (Smith 1997; Watson 1997). This provided an opportunity, documented below, to compare the abundance of craneflies with bird numbers and breeding success.

Results

Breeding success of birds in relation to cranefly score

Table 1 shows data on the breeding success of golden plover and dotterel at Glas Maol, and on cranefly scores. Golden plover reared more young per adult than dotterel. The clutch was generally four eggs as against the dotterel's three, and both sexes took part in parental care, whereas typically only cock dotterel did so. The range in breeding success between years was large in both species.

At Glas Maol, the breeding success of golden plover and of dotterel was positively correlated with the cranefly score in the same summer (Table 2). The relationship was stronger in golden plover. Breeding success of dotterel at Cairn Gorm was associated positively with the cranefly score (Table 2). However, unlike that at Glas Maol, the relationship at Cairn Gorm was not significant.

Demographic comparisons of golden plover and dotterel

The breeding success of golden plover at Glas Maol was correlated positively with that of dotterel over the whole run of years ($n = 41$, $r_s = 0.359$, $P = 0.022$), but not significantly for years up to 1987 inclusive ($n = 23$, $r_s = 0.357$, $P = 0.09$) before a marked decline of golden plover occurred up to 1988 and since. Golden plover tend to lay eggs earlier in the year than dotterel, but take longer to lay a clutch, incubate eggs, and hatch and rear chicks. Hence they and dotterel may be affected differently by weather, the timing and concentration of the cranefly emergence, and predation.

Breeding success of golden plover and dotterel in relation to calendar year

During years up to 1987 inclusive, before a long-term decline in numbers occurred, the breeding success of golden plover at Glas Maol did not change in relation to the calendar year ($n = 27$, $r_s = 0.007$, $P = 0.97$). Over the run of years up to 2012 as a whole, it showed a negative tendency, but very slight and far from significant ($n = 52$, $r_s = -0.20$, $P = 0.16$).

The breeding success of dotterel at Glas Maol tended to decrease up to 1987 ($n = 23$, $r_s = -0.353$, $P = 0.098$), but again far from significantly. In the entire run of years the decrease was apparently slightly less ($n = 42$, $r_s = -0.277$, $P = 0.076$).

Breeding success of golden plover in relation to May rainfall measured at Braemar

The reason for considering rainfall was that the wet, poorly drained places favoured by feeding adult and young golden plover remain wet during Mays with heavy rainfall, whereas in Mays of little rainfall they dry up, even including pools. Breeding success of golden plover on Glas Maol proved to be positively correlated with May rainfall at Braemar ($n = 52$, $r = 0.332$, $P = 0.016$). The cranefly score was also correlated positively with May rainfall at Braemar ($n = 52$, $r_s = 0.283$, $P = 0.042$), though less strongly.

Discussion

It should be noted that May rainfall at Braemar accounted for only a small proportion of the variation in breeding success at Glas Maol, so other factors are obviously important. One confounding factor was that the melting of an extensive snow cover in May can contribute massively to wet ground and pools, even though rainfall may be low.

The breeding success of golden plover on Glas Maol exceeded that recorded in Parr's (1990a & b, 1992 a & b) intensive study on Kerloch moor. The number of young reared per adult present in spring on Kerloch varied from 0.2 to 2.0 (mean 0.85) in years of increasing or stable numbers, but fell steeply to 0–0.5 (mean 0.06) in years when the population declined to extinction.

Parr (1992a, b) stated that breeding success on Caithness blanket bog exceeded that on Kerloch. His measure of breeding success in Caithness was the proportion of pairs that reared young, not the number of young reared per pair. Nonetheless, this proportion was 94–97% (Parr 1990b, 1992), and so nest losses must have been very small.

Byrkjedal (1987) reported a mean of 0.53 fledged young per nest over seven summers on an alpine area in south Norway. Nest losses to predators (78% in golden plover and 47% in dotterel) far exceeded those noted in Scotland. It seems possible that repeated visits to nests in the Norwegian study induced unnaturally high predation. No check on this, by work on a control area without nest visits or with less frequent visits, was reported.

References

Byrkjedal, I. (1980). Summer food of the golden plover *Pluvialis apricaria* at Hardangervidda, south Norway. Holarctic Ecology 3, 40–49.

Byrkjedal, I. (1987). Antipredator behavior and breeding success in greater golden-plover and Eurasian dotterel. Condor 89, 40–47.

Galbraith, H., Murray, S., Duncan, K., Smith, R., Whitfield, D.P. & Thompson, D.B.A. (1993). Diet and habitat use of the dotterel (*Charadrius morinellus*) in Scotland. Ibis 135, 148–155.

Hofsvang, T. (1972). *Tipula excisa* Schum. (Diptera, Tipulidae), life cycle and population dynamics. Norsk Entomologisk Tidsskrift 19, 43–48.

Holt, S. & Whitfield, D.P. (1996a). Montane Ecology Project site report series: Cairn Gorm study area. Scottish Natural Heritage, Edinburgh.

Holt, S. & Whitfield, D.P. (1996b). Montane Ecology Project site report series: Glas Maol, Eastern Grampians. Scottish Natural Heritage, Edinburgh.

Shaw, P., Thompson, D.B.A., Duncan, K. & Buxton, N. (2006). Birds. In: The nature of the Cairngorms: diversity in a changing environment (Ed. by P. Shaw & D.B.A. Thompson), 293–339.

Smith, R.M. (1997). Ecology of the crane-fly *Tipula montana* in an upland environment. PhD thesis, University of Aberdeen.

Thompson, D.B.A. & Whitfield, D.P. (1993). Research progress report. Scottish Birds 17, 1–8.

Thompson, D.B.A., Whitfield, D.P., Galbraith, H., Duncan, K., Smith, R.D., Murray, S. & Holt, S. (2003). Breeding bird assemblages and habitat use of alpine areas in Scotland. In: Alpine biodiversity in Europe (Ed. by L. Nagy, G. Grabherr, C. Korner & DBA Thompson), 327–338. Springer-Verlag, Berlin & Heidelberg.

Watson, A. (1965). A population study of ptarmigan (*Lagopus mutus*) in Scotland. Journal of Animal Ecology 34, 135–172.

Watson, A. (1981). Detailed analysis. Lurcher's Gully Public Inquiry, Kingussie.

Watson, A. (1988). Dotterel *Charadrius morinellus* numbers in relation to human impact in Scotland. Biological Conservation 43, 245–256.

Watson, A. (1989). Dotterel populations and spacing on three Scottish areas in 1967-86. Ornis Fennica 66, 85–99.

Watson, A. (1996). Human-induced increases of carrion crows and gulls on Cairngorms plateaux. Scottish Birds 18, 206–213.

Watson, A. (1997). Habitat use by snow buntings in Scotland from spring to autumn. Scottish Birds 19, 105–113.

Watson, A. & O'Hare, P.J. (1979). Spacing behaviour of red grouse at low density on Irish bog. Ornis Scandinavica 10, 252–261.

Watson, A. & Rae, R. (1987). Dotterel numbers, habitat and breeding success in Scotland. Scottish Birds 14, 191–198.

Table 1. Mean, standard error of the mean, and range for breeding success and for the score of cranefly abundance.

Area	Parameter	n years	Mean, SE	Range
Glas Maol	Golden plover young/old	52	0.830, 0.059	0.00–1.87
	Dotterel young/old	41	0.627, 0.053	0.00–1.25
	Cranefly score	52	2.577, 0.213	1–5
Cairn Gorm	Dotterel young/spring cock	36	0.305, 0.033	0.0–0.75
	Cranefly score	29	2.414, .0.251	1–4

Table 2. Correlation coefficients (r_s) between breeding success (number of young reared per adult) and the score for cranefly abundance in the same summer.

Area	Breeding success	r_s	n years	P
Glas Maol	Golden plover young/old	0.742	52	<0.0001
	Dotterel young/spring cock	0.344	41	0.028
Cairn Gorm	Dotterel young/spring cock*	0.405	17	0.106

* From 2000 onwards I did not know cock numbers in spring, so I express breeding success as the number of young/cock in late summer. Because this was different, I exclude it in the above analysis.

Moorland converted to agricultural grassland at Pitreadie farm, Kerloch, near Banchory, September 1963

Chapter 4. Abundance of breeding golden plover within and amongst areas

Summary

During decades when no long-term rise or fall in spring densities of golden plover (*Pluvialis apricaria*) occurred, numbers on several areas of lower moorland were positively correlated with one another, but not with numbers on an area of high peaty moorland, and generally not with numbers on alpine land.

In the Cairngorms massif, numbers on three alpine areas were negatively correlated with the incidence of prolonged snow-lie from snowfalls in early summer. This did not apply to alpine land on the lower hill of Glas Maol, where summer snowfalls were scarcer, lighter and more ephemeral than in the Cairngorms.

On several study areas with long runs of data, the proportionate change in number from spring $i-1$ to spring i (for brevity called change in number) was correlated with weather at climatological stations. Correlations were positive with mean monthly temperature in January, February and March at Leuchars airport on east-coastal lowland where birds colour-ringed on Deeside are known to winter, negative with the number of winter days with air frost at Leuchars, and negative with the number of winter mornings with snow lying at Braemar village near some of the study areas. The obvious interpretation is that cold snowy weather causes more deaths of birds on the wintering grounds..

At Glas Maol, change in number was correlated positively with breeding success in the intervening summer $i-1$, and negatively with adult density in spring $i-1$. Breeding success in summer i was negatively correlated with adult density in spring i, so that density apparently had a negative effect on breeding success.

On other areas there were no good data on breeding success. As at Glas Maol, however, change in number at other areas was negatively correlated with the number in spring $i-1$. Hence, for example, change in number was lower when density in the previous spring had been high.

Mean differences in density amongst areas accompanied differences in topography and vegetation. No birds were found breeding on steep slopes or on extensive smooth agricultural grassland such as old abandoned fields and currently managed fields. Mean densities on different areas of low moorland were correlated negatively with the mean height of heather, the higher densities being on ground with short heather due to burning and heavy grazing. There was some evidence of mean density being greater on moorland near grass fields, which the adults used for feeding before and during the breeding season. Densities on moorland and alpine land over base-rich bedrock exceeded those over poorer rocks, soils on the latter being more acidic.

In experiments where fertiliser was applied to heather moorland for research on red grouse, the density of golden plover showed no material difference before and after the application. Likewise it did not differ there relative to control areas.

Introduction

This paper compares annual fluctuations

in numbers of breeding golden plover on study areas, mostly in north-east Scotland. These included alpine land, high moorland, and lower moorland. On one alpine area I recorded breeding success, and so could compare change in numbers from spring to spring there with breeding success in the intervening summer. The time-span of observations varied greatly on different areas, with the longest run spanning 1944–2012, and the shortest in only one year.

Study areas

All study areas were chosen for other purposes, almost all for population studies of red grouse (*Lagopus lagopus scoticus*) on moorland or ptarmigan (*Lagopus mutus*) on alpine land. They are listed in Tables 1 and 2. The surface area in hectares, range of altitude, map grid reference, and main type of bedrock have been published for most areas (Jenkins *et al*. 1963, 1967; Watson *et al*. 1977; Watson 1989; Jenkins & Watson 2001), along with descriptions of the areas and their features. Alpine areas at Cairn Gorm, Beinn a' Bhuird and Glas Maol were Areas A, B and C in descriptions by Watson (1989), and further description is in Chapter 4. An alpine area at lower altitude was on Carn nan Sac near Carn a' Gheoidh west of Glas Maol, described in Watson *et al*. (1998).

Methods

On moorland, adult numbers were counted using pointing dogs trained in searching the ground for counts of red grouse and ptarmigan. On some areas, birds were counted from a land rover used as a mobile hide, in the course of prolonged watches of territorial behaviour in red grouse, a method described by Watson & Miller (1971). On alpine areas, dogs were used for most counts, but I did some by walking slowly without dogs, finding birds by scanning with binoculars as in counts of dotterel (Watson & Rae 1987; Watson 1988, 1989). Adult golden plover are very conspicuous and easily seen on the short prostrate vegetation of Scottish alpine ground, except when sitting on nests and downy chicks. A few counts on moorland and alpine areas were checked by listening to birds singing during the dusk or dawn chorus. All three methods produced repeatable reliable counts when tested against one another, and also on areas at Kerloch moor where many birds were individually marked for Parr's more intensive study of the species (Watson & O'Hare 1979a, b; Parr 1990, 1992a, b; Chapter 3).

When golden plover return to the breeding grounds they arrive in flocks (Parr 1990). Birds that breed on moorland feed in flocks, mostly on short grass in fields (Parr 1990), whereas alpine birds forage in flocks on snow-free short vegetation. Pairs then disperse on territories, but often re-join flocks for foraging later in the same day, and some do this during the periods of incubation and chick-rearing. Adults and fledged young form flocks in late summer along with adults that have failed. Moorland birds in late summer tend to leave the area as soon as adults have failed or their young are fledged, but on alpine land they tend to stay in flocks for some weeks or even months. On both kinds of area, the last few birds to remain are occasionally single lone juveniles (Parr 1990; A. Watson unpublished).

Many birds that lose their nests will re-lay and rear broods that are several weeks later than the rest. Also, Parr (1990) recorded frequent sequential breeding at Kerloch moor, where some birds in waiting flocks paired and bred on territories after the earlier territorial residents had bred successfully or had failed and then rejoined the flock. If observers make only one visit to check breeding success in late summer, late birds may still be on eggs or with downy chicks. However, such birds are easily detected because of their alarm calls and other alarm behaviour, and extra later visits will show whether they have been successful in rearing young, and, if so, how many.

Data on weather came from climatological stations at Leuchars airport and Braemar, supervised by the Meteorological Office (Monthly Weather Report, Bracknell). I used the monthly mean air temperature at Leuchars for certain winter months, the number of winter days with air frost at Leuchars, and the number of days with snow lying at Braemar in each winter season from October to April. The criterion for snow-lie by the Snow Survey of Great Britain is that snow covers >50% of the ground at 0900 hours (Meteorological Office, Bracknell). Parr (1992b) gave evidence that golden plover which bred at Kerloch on Deeside spent the midwinter on coastal farmland in Angus before returning to the breeding grounds in February. The coastal farmland lay north of the Tay estuary and Leuchars was on similar farmland south of the estuary. It is well known in meteorology that the directions of differences between winters at any one place such as Braemar are shared regionally and nationally.

On nine moorland areas in north-east Scotland and one in Co Mayo, some or all ground was fertilised in experiments to test hypotheses about nutrition and populations of red grouse (Watson *et al.* 1977; Watson & O'Hare 1979c). This afforded a useful opportunity to find whether the spring densities of golden plover responded. At three Scottish areas, fertiliser was applied to all the ground as calcium ammonium nitrate, on one of the areas along with ground mineral phosphate, and at three areas it was ground mineral phosphate without nitrate. At three other Scottish areas, nitrate was applied in strips, at one area a third of the ground being treated, and at the other two a fifth. At an area in Co Mayo, the treatment involved fencing to exclude sheep and cattle, phosphate applied to large plots, and shallow ditches in the plots. A Scottish area with a phosphate treatment was also fenced to exclude sheep and cattle. The experiments increased the heather's growth and nutritive value, except at the Scottish experiments with phosphate.

Results
Are spring numbers of golden plover on different areas correlated?
Moorland
It seemed reasonable to expect that numbers on adjacent or nearby areas at similar altitude would be positively correlated with one another, and that this might perhaps apply to distant areas at a broadly similar altitude. Numbers on three adjacent sub-areas of high moorland at the Glen Esk high area were correlated positively with one another over the four years of study (numbers on area A compared with B, $r = 0.970$, $P = 0.030$; A with C, $r = 0.962$, $P = 0.038$; and B with C, $r = 0.980$, $P = 0.020$).

This did not apply at the different sub-areas on Glen Esk low area, although it came within 1 km of the high area, albeit at lower altitude. However, the low area had been divided for grouse studies into a larger number of mostly smaller sub-areas, and hence there was a greater likelihood of some pairs straddling the boundary between two sub-areas, leading to greater variability in any one sub-area. Also, the low area had a greater diversity of landforms and soils even within any one sub-area, creating a more intricate fine-grained pattern, such as glacial hillocks and ridges, a tarn, alluvium, prehistoric field-systems, arable fields, permanent pasture fields, and many groundwater flushes. The high area had none of these, apart from alluvium and flushes, but the extent of alluvium on the low area far exceeded that on the high area, because of streams being larger.

When I compared numbers on lower moorland with totals on all of the sub-areas of the high area, again the two were not correlated. The high area stood out as materially different from all the moorland areas at low and intermediate altitude, in its extensive blanket peat covering much of the ground, separated by exposed broad ridges with eroded peat and patches of bare soil.

It seemed that habitat type was relevant, not altitude. Numbers even on distant areas of moorland at low and intermediate altitudes tended to be correlated positively with one another (Tables 3, 4, 5).

Furthermore, when numbers on lower moorland were compared with numbers on alpine land, the lack of correlation with numbers on the peaty moorland of the High area was accentuated further. It became a negative association in most cases.

Alpine land
On alpine land, spring numbers at Beinn a' Bhuird, Cairn Lochan and Derry Cairngorm were positively correlated (Table 6). Numbers on the alpine base-rich Glas Maol, however, were not associated with numbers on the other three hills, which stood at higher altitudes, and overlay infertile granitic bedrock.

The incidence of late snow cover on alpine land was correlated negatively with spring numbers on Beinn a' Bhuird, Cairn Lochan and Derry Cairngorm (n = 20, 43 and 44 years, r_s = –0.697, –0.500 and –0.610, P = 0.0009, 0.0008 and <0.0001). I had to use spring numbers rather than proportionate change for these three areas, because there were so many years with no birds.

At Glas Maol, where birds occurred in all years, I could use proportionate change because birds occurred in all years. Change was only weakly associated with the incidence of late snow (n = 33 years, r_s = –0.260, P = 0.14), as was the number of birds (n = 35, r_s = 0.105, P = 0.5). This evident lesser influence was associated with Glas Maol being far less affected by late snowfalls than the three higher-altitude and more northerly hills in the Cairngorms.

Proportionate change in numbers and density in relation to breeding success
One question was whether breeding success affected change in spring numbers between years, with the expectation that good breeding would lead to a rise in spring numbers, and poor breeding to a decline. This was tested with data from Glas Maol, where there was a long run of counts of golden plover and of records of their breeding success. Change in number from spring $i–1$ to spring i was correlated positively with breeding success in summer $i–1$ during years up to a marked decline

Flock of 2000 golden plover on permanent pasture, St Fergus near Loch of Strathbeg, 24 October 1976

in 1987–88 (Table 7). This was evidence that breeding success may drive change in numbers. Since 1988, however, when numbers have been much lower and in some years just one pair, the association became negative, though far from significant ($n = 25$ years, $r_s = -0.268$, $P = 0.20$).

A second question was whether change in number, and separately the density in spring i, affected breeding success in summer i. Change in number and spring density proved to be negatively correlated with breeding success (Table 7). This was evidence for a possible density-dependent relationship where breeding success tends to be lower in a summer after spring numbers have risen. Hence this appears to be a possible mechanism for regulating numbers between years.

Proportionate change in spring numbers in relation to density

The question here was whether the number of birds in spring $i-1$ affected the subsequent proportionate change in number. Because this did not involve breeding success, data were available at other study areas besides Glas Maol. The expectation was that a high density in the previous year would tend to be followed by a fall in numbers, and a low density to be followed by a rise. There was evidence of this from a study in the Peak District of England, where change in numbers was related negatively to the number of adults in spring $i-1$ (Yalden & Pearce-Higgins 1997).

In the present study also, change in number from spring $i-1$ to spring i proved to be correlated negatively with the number in spring $i-1$ (Table 7). Number in this case was equivalent to density within a given study area, because the size of study areas remained unchanged throughout. Hence the above result provided evidence of a possible density-dependent mechanism for regulating numbers.

Proportionate change in spring numbers amongst years in relation to weather

Frost and snow on the birds' wintering grounds might reduce their survival and so reduce the number returning to the nesting grounds Parr (1992b). Moreover, Yalden & Pearce-Higgins (1997) found that change in number was related positively to winter temperature.

In the present study I used change in number at several areas with long runs of data on bird numbers, and compared these with weather data at Leuchars airport in Fife and at Braemar village. Change in number proved to be correlated positively with mean monthly air temperatures in winter at Leuchars, and negatively with the number of winter days of air frost at Leuchars (Table 8). At Glas Maol, change in number was correlated negatively with April temperature at nearby Braemar ($n = 33$ years, $r = -0.552$, $P = 0.0009$). Because April is probably past the period of winter food shortage, one might infer from this correlation that birds settle to a lesser extent on alpine land in cold snowy springs.

At Glenamoy in Co Mayo, western Ireland, Watson & O' Hare (1979b) found a positive correlation ($r = 0.67$) between mean temperature in June and the number of golden plover in the next year, though not significant because of only four years of data. Presumably the likely effect would operate via better breeding success in warm Junes, and more young leading to an increase next spring.

In the present study I compared change in number from year $i-1$ to year i with the mean air temperature for June $i-1$ at Braemar. There was a positive correlation with change in number at Glas Maol ($n = 31$, $r_s = 0.387$, $P = 0.032$) and at Glen Esk V+VIa ($n = 14$, $r_s = 0.465$, $P = 0.035$). At Corndavon and Abergeldie it was positive, but far from significant, There was, however, a stronger correlation at nearby Glen Muick ($n = 13$, $r_s = 0.598$, $P = 0.031$). Benign weather might well differ between the very wet climate of Glenamoy and the more continental climate in north-east Scotland. For example, a very warm June in eastern Scotland might result in surface soil being too dry for chicks to find invertebrate food.

Mean densities varying amongst areas

The questions here are whether mean density in spring varies amongst different areas, and if so, whether such variation is associated with habitat features. Mean density varied much between different areas (Tables 1 and 2).

Mean density on moorland and alpine land was associated with topography and vegetation. I found no birds on steep slopes (Appendix). On moorland I saw none breeding on large expanses of short grazed grass on old abandoned fields nearby, or on currently enclosed fields nearby, although moorland birds often flew to both kinds of fields to feed on earthworms and smaller invertebrate items.

At areas on heather moorland, golden plover did not occur on heather that was tall because of little or no burning and grazing. There was some evidence that birds colonised areas where tall heather later became shorter due to burning or grazing. Likewise, I found some evidence that they deserted areas where previously short heather had grown tall because of lack of burning or grazing.

These observations indicated that vegetation height may affect the birds' abundance. In a study of the food supply of red grouse, the height and age of heather were measured in 1958–61 on 15 heather-dominated moorland areas in north-east Scotland, along with the proportion of the ground covered by heather (Miller et al. 1966). I have now compared these independent data with the mean density of golden plover in spring 1958–61 on the same 15 areas. The age and height of the heather were correlated negatively and significantly with plover density amongst these moorland study areas, the percentage cover also negative but far from significant (Table 9).

At Kerloch, parts I and V were fenced for research on red grouse, with cattle and sheep excluded. Golden plover declined on V (Table 10). On part I, many patches of heather were burned in 1962–65, the now ungrazed heather increased in height on the rest of the area, no burning took place in 1966, and only a tiny fire in 1967 (Miller et al. 1970). The birds at first maintained their 1961 numbers through to 1965, and then declined to one third of this in 1966 and thereafter, thus showing an overall decline (Table 10). They increased on other low areas at similar altitude, where fences were not erected to exclude sheep and cattle. There, heavy grazing by sheep and cattle reduced the height of heather and kept it short without any burning (Welch 1984), on parts III, XI, and the lower sections of II and IV. At higher altitude on II and IV, further from the farms, grazing was less heavy and the heather increased in height, but rotational burning was done. Hence birds declined where the heather height increased.

Other features associated with mean differences in density are described in the Appendix. The low area at Glen Esk held a larger density than the nearby high area, associated with many grass fields on fertile cultivated or formerly cultivated soils, where birds fed frequently. The areas at Corndavon and the Strone also held among the largest densities of the moorland areas and again lay beside grass fields.

In addition, a separate study in 2003–10 involving soil profiles has shown that large sections of heather moorland on and adjacent to the Glen Esk low area, the Strone and nearby land close to the Corndavon area, and at Pitcarmick contain fertile soils with herb-rich heather and unusually many earthworms and moles for heather-dominated moorland, following prehistoric human agriculture and settlement (Watson *et al.* 2010). Smaller patches of heather-dominated moorland at Abergeldie also show soils with evidence of former cultivation, along with remains of corn-kilns and houses from a more recent period since the Middle Ages.

Another question is whether density over base-rich bedrock exceeds that over poorer rocks. I classified the richness of underlying bedrock following suggestions made by an expert geologist in Watson & Moss (2008, their Table 24 and notes below it). This classification involved three types, poor, intermediate and rich, examples of poor being granite and quartzite, and of rich being limestone and calc-schist. None of my alpine study areas lay on rich rock and almost no moorland ones, so there was no point in treating them separately. Therefore I combined them with intermediate areas. For statistical analysis I excluded study areas in regions with a radically different climate from the bulk of my study areas in north-east Scotland, such as oceanic areas in the western and west-central Highlands and western Ireland, and in south Scotland beside the English border, and also on the blown sand at Sands of Forvie by the North Sea near Aberdeen. Because golden plover generally avoid steep slopes for breeding, I excluded a few alpine areas with steep slopes, such as my study areas for ptarmigan on the Cairnwell and Meall Odhar at Glenshee Ski Centre.

The analysis showed that mean densities over poor bedrock were lower than those over richer rock, on alpine areas ($n = 7$ and 10, means 3.44 ± standard error of the mean 1.23, and 9.81 ± 1.36, two-sample $T = 3.30$, $P = 0.005$). This was on the assumption that variances were equal, as indicated by an F test where the probability was not significant (folded $F = 1.76$ and $P = 0.25$). This difference held also for moorland over poor and richer bedrocks ($n = 57$ and 40, means 6.30 ± 0.60 and 8.69 ± 0.78, two-sample $T = 2.47$, $P = 0.0152$). This involved the assumption that variances were equal, the probability for the F test being far from significant (folded $F = 1.20$, $P = 0.26$).

Lack of response to experiments with fertilisers

Within each of the 10 pairs of areas I compared density on the experimental area with that on the control in the spring before fertiliser was applied. The mean density on the areas to be fertilised was 8.39

birds per 100 ha (SE 1.62), whereas that on the control was 7.00 (1.09), in other words slightly more on the areas to be fertilised. A paired test showed no significant difference ($T = 0.91$, $P = 0.39$). Hence, the experimental and control areas formed comparable pairs before the experiment.

Next I calculated the proportionate change in number between the spring before fertilising and the first spring after fertilising, and compared this with the mean proportionate change in number for all years of subsequent counts up to three years, on each experimental area relative to its paired control. In the 10 pairs of areas, a paired test showed no difference ($T = 0.97$, $P = 0.36$).

In short, the evidence indicated no material response to fertilising. It is possible that factors which increase the height of the vegetation, such as fertiliser or lack of grazing or shelter from trees, might have adverse effects on numbers. In the above cases, only the fence in Co Mayo proved effective against surreptitious opening by farmers. On the other nine areas, sheep and cattle increased relative to the control (Watson *et al*. 1977), and their heavier grazing prevented the heather from becoming materially taller.

Discussion

Fluctuations in spring numbers

The proportionate change in number of golden plover on each of the high alpine areas in the Cairngorms massif was negatively correlated with the incidence of late snow there. In years of late snow, frequently no birds were found. This suggests that fewer birds may decide to settle in summers with extensive late snow.

Fluctuations in spring numbers were correlated positively amongst different areas of lower moorland. However, they were poorly associated when numbers on these areas were compared with those on high moorland, and even negatively associated when compared with numbers on alpine areas. It is unknown whether such differences may be due to lower areas being core habitats that involve emigrants to higher areas in certain years, or vice versa.

At Glas Maol, the only area where I had a good run of data on breeding success, change in number from one spring to the next was correlated positively with breeding success in the intervening summer. This occurred during years up to a marked decline of spring numbers between 1987 and 1988. A reasonable inference is that breeding success is one factor that can contribute to driving spring numbers. The association became negative in years after 1988, however, when spring numbers have been much lower and in some years only one pair. In the later set of years, this might suggest that net movement of adults to Glas Maol contributed to maintaining spring numbers.

Breeding success

I was unable to obtain reasonably large samples of data on breeding success except on Glas Maol, where short alpine vegetation made this possible. On moorland study areas, many broods of fledged young were seen during counts of red grouse with dogs and occasionally during counts from a land rover. However, even big chicks could readily hide in the taller vegetation, and during the counts of red grouse I was unable to obtain good data on breeding success of moorland curlew and snipe for the same reason.

By concentrating some effort on counts of moorland golden plover without the main aim being to count red grouse, Parr (1980) was able to find the number of young reared per successful brood as well as the number of nests robbed by predators. His annual means for the number of fledged young per successful pair varied from 1.33 to 2.00, with an overall mean of 1.53. Breeding success on Glas Maol exceeded that on Parr's study area at Kerloch moor, even during the years when Parr's population had not yet started to decline.

I compared these findings with my notes on breeding success from all study areas other than Glas Maol, and from all years. Unfortunately I often did not note the numbers. On four alpine areas the total noted was 32 young reared in 20 successful broods, with the number in a brood varying from 1 to 4. On three moorland areas, the relevant values were 28 young reared in 20 successful broods varying from 1 in a brood to 4. I have no data on the number of failed broods on moorland. Statistical analysis of this apparent difference would be dubious, because the years with recorded alpine data differed from those for moorland. Parr appears to be the only person who has produced good data on this parameter for golden plover on Scottish moorland. A recent intensive study in the Peak District by Pearce-Higgins & Yalden (2003), who used radio-telemetry, revealed a mean of 1.31 fledglings per successful brood, and an estimated 0.57 fledglings per pair.

Differences in mean densities amongst areas

In a comparison of 15 moorland study areas in north-east Scotland, the height of the heather accounted for much of the variation in the mean density of golden plover over several years, with higher densities on areas with shorter heather (Results). On a larger number of moorland areas in south Scotland and north England, where survey on a given area covered one season, the density of golden plover was again related negatively to the height of dwarf shrubs, mostly comprising heather (Pearce-Higgins & Grant 2006).

Mean densities on the low area at Glen Esk exceeded those on the nearby high area. The high area had big expanses of blanket bog, the low area none. Flushes were more numerous and larger on the low than on the high area. Adults and young avoided large moorland flushes with perennial flowing water, which supported tall vegetation such as rushes and bog myrtle (see Appendix). However, these large flushes would have contributed nutrient enrichment to freely drained moorland beside them. Also, the low area had many small flushes where water flowed on the surface only after heavy rain, and golden plover with their chicks often foraged there.

The low area had a far larger number of small patches of smooth short grass within the heather moorland, associated with heavier grazing and dunging by sheep and cattle, as well as with more rabbits. The different parts of the low area lay around some grass fields that were grazed by sheep and cattle, and that were frequently visited for feeding on earthworms by adult golden plover from the low area and in flocks from outside. Hence the close vicinity of grazed grass fields may have boosted the habitat quality of the low area.

Statistical analysis showed that mean densities on study areas over base-rich bedrocks exceeded those over poor bedrocks, on alpine land and moorland. Soils over richer rocks have thicker horizons of humus and other upper soil horizons, and a more cohesive structure with smaller particles. Hard acidic rocks such as granite break down into large loose in-cohesive particles, and hold low contents of chemical elements important for plant growth, such as calcium and phosphorus (e.g. Johnstone 1974). On his page 208, Johnstone gave a good brief summary of how 'The crystalline structure and chemical composition of the rocks affect vegetation and animal life'. It seems likely that soils which have developed over richer rocks support a greater abundance and variety of invertebrates than soils over poorer rocks. This might be a reason for attracting higher densities of golden plover.

References

Jenkins, D., Watson, A. & Miller, G.R. (1963). Population studies on red grouse, *Lagopus lagopus scoticus* (Lath.) in north-east Scotland. Journal of Animal Ecology 32, 317–376.

Jenkins, D., Watson, A. & Miller, G.R. (1967). Population fluctuations in the red grouse *Lagopus lagopus scoticus*. Journal of Animal Ecology 36, 97–122.

Jenkins, D. & Watson, A. (2001). Bird numbers in relation to grazing on a grouse moor from 1957–61 to 1988–98. Bird Study 48, 18–22.

Johnstone, G.S. (1974). Geology. In: The Cairngorms, by D. Nethersole-Thompson & A. Watson, 200–209. Collins, London.

Miller, G.R., Jenkins, D. & Watson, A. (1966). Heather performance and red grouse populations. I. Visual estimates of heather performance. Journal of Applied Ecology 3, 313–326.

Miller, G. R., Jenkins, D. & Watson, A. (1970). Responses of red grouse populations to experimental improvement of their food. Animal populations in relation to their food resources (Ed. by A. Watson), pp. 323–335. Blackwell Scientific Publications, Oxford.

Moss, R., Elston, D.A. & Watson, A. (2000). Spatial asynchrony and demographic travelling waves during red grouse population cycles. Ecology 81, 981–989.

Parr, R. (1980). Population study of golden plover *Pluvialis apricaria* using marked birds. Ornis Scandinavica 11, 179–189.

Parr, R.A. (1992a). Moorland birds and their predators in relation to afforestation. PhD thesis, University of Aberdeen.

Parr, R. (1992b). The decline to extinction of a population of golden plover in north-east Scotland. Ornis Scandinavica 23, 152–158.

Parr, R. (1993). Nest predation and numbers of golden plovers *Pluvialis apricaria* and other moorland waders. Bird Study 40, 223–231.

Pearce-Higgins, J. & Grant, M.C. (2006). Relationships between bird abundance and the composition and structure of moorland vegetation. Bird Study 53, 112–125.

Pearce-Higgins, J. & Yalden,D.W. (2003). Golden plover *Pluvialis apricaria* breeding success and on a moor managed for shooting red grouse *Lagopus lagopus*. Bird Study 50, 170–177.

Watson, A. (1965). A population study of ptarmigan (*Lagopus mutus*) in Scotland. Journal of Animal Ecology

Watson, A. (1988). Dotterel *Charadrius morinellus* numbers in relation to human impact in Scotland. Biological Conservation 43, 245–256.

Watson, A. (1989). Dotterel populations and spacing on three Scottish areas in 1967–86. Ornis Fennica 66, 85–99.

Watson, A. & Miller, G.R. (1971). Territory size and aggression in a fluctuating red grouse population. Journal of Animal Ecology 40, 367–383.

Watson, A. & O'Hare, P.J. (1979a). Spacing behaviour of red grouse at low density on Irish bog. Ornis Scandinavica 10, 252–261.

Watson, A. & Moss, R. (2008). Grouse. Collins, London.

Watson, A., Moss, R. & Parr, R. (1987). Grouse increase on Mull. Landowning in Scotland 207, 6.

Watson, A., Moss, R., Phillips, J. & Parr, R. (1977). The effect of fertilizers on red grouse stocks on Scottish moors grazed by sheep, cattle and deer. In: Écologie du petit gibier et aménagement des chasses (Ed. by P. Pesson), 193–212. Gauthier-Villars, Paris.

Watson, A., Moss, R. & Rae, S. (1998). Population dynamics of Scottish rock ptarmigan cycles. Ecology 79, 1174–1192.

Watson, A. & O'Hare, P.J. (1979b). Bird and mammal numbers on untreated and experimentally treated Irish bog. Oikos 33, 97–105.

Watson, A. & O'Hare, P.J. (1979c). Red grouse populations on experimentally treated and untreated Irish bog. Journal of Applied Ecology 16, 433–452.

Watson, A., Walker, A.D., Heslop, R.E. (2010). Research by three biologist colleagues with Ian Shepherd. In: A Lad o' Pairts: a Day Conference in Memory of Ian Shepherd (Ed. by Moira Greig), 60–62. Aberdeenshire Council, Aberdeen.

Welch, D. (1984). Studies in the grazing of heather moorland in north-east Scotland. II. Responses of heather. Journal of Applied Ecology 21, 197–207.

Yalden, D.W. & Pearce-Higgins, J.W. (1997). Density-dependence and winter weather as factors affecting the size of a population of golden plovers. Bird Study 44, 227–234.

Table 1. Numbers on areas surveyed only once, top 11 rows alpine, others moorland. In Tables 1 and 2, the column headed Rock shows whether the underlying bedrock is poor, intermediate, or rich, based on Watson & Moss (2008, Table 24 and its notes), with 1 representing poor, 2 intermediate and 3 rich.

	Ha	Rock	Year	No per 100 ha
Wester Ross, Maoile Lunndaidh	40	1	1954	2.5
Newtonmore, A' Chailleach	100	2	1954	4.0
Newtonmore, Carn Sgulain	100	2	1954	4.0
Durness, Farrmheall	100	1	1960	2.0
Durness, Creag Riabhach	50	1	1960	2.0
Sutherland, Ben Klibreck	50	2	1960	12.0
Ben Avon, Carn Eas	100	1	1962	8.0
Glas Maol, White Brae	80	2	1987	10.0
Glas Maol, Druim Mor	100	2	1987	8.0
Little Glas Maol	50	2	1987	8.0
Meall a' Bhuiridh, Coire Pollach	75	1	1996	5.3
Moray, Castle Grant, Badahad	50	1	1956	8.0
Kinlochbervie, Strath Shinary	200	1	1958	0.5
Wester Ross, Kishorn, Couldoran	134	1	1959	1.5
Roar Hill	118	2	1959	7.6
Glenshee Lodge	120	2	1960	6.7
Tongue, Loch an Dherue	100	1	1960	4.0
Tongue, A' Mhoine	100	1	1960	2.0
Tongue, Kinloch	100	1	1960	4.0
Durness, Rhigolter	100	1	1960	2.0
Durness, Inshore	100	1	1960	4.0
Durness, Sandwood	100	1	1960	2.0
Durness, Gualin	100	1	1960	2.0
Kinlochbervie, Rhiconich	100	1	1960	2.0
Durness, Ceannabeinne	100	1	1960	2.0
Kerloch, South Dennetys	190	2	1961	3.2
Moray, Elchies south	125	1	1962	1.6

Moray, Elchies north	125	1	1962	1.6
Banchory, Tilquhillie, south	100	2	1963	2.0
Banchory, Tilquhillie, north	50	2	1963	4.0
Dinnet, Morven, above Stotwell	100	2	1964	2.0
Moray, Altyre north	20	1	1964	10.0
Moray, Altyre south	20	1	1964	10.0
Co Mayo, Glenamoy, Meenard north	130	1	1967	2.3
Co Mayo, Glenamoy, Keenagh	130	1	1967	0
Langholm west	87	3	1969	0
Langholm east	80	3	1969	5.0
Cromdale, Carn Tuairneir	42	1	1971	9.9
Cromdale, Glenlochy west	90	1	1971	8.9
Cromdale, Glenlochy east	50	1	1971	8.0
Glen Livet, Thain	100	1	1974	12.0
Glen Gairn, Scraulac	200	2	1974	18.0
Correen Hills, The Suie	100	2	1974	12.0
Cromdale, Carn Eachie	135	1	1975	11.9
Duthil, The Cam Sgriob south	100	1	1975	10.0
Mull, Torloisk area G	302	2	1980	0.7
Glen Gairn, Easter Sleach	100	2	1981	14.0
Abergeldie, The Genechal	100	1	1981	12.0
Glen Gairn, Cnoc Chalmac	100	2	1981	14.0
Glen Gairn, Carn a' Bhacain	125	1	1988	8.0
Melvich, Lochstrathy	100	1	1988	4.0
Melvich, The Yellow Bog	50	1	1988	4.0
Ladder Hills, Little Geal Charn	100	2	1988	10.0
Ladder Hills, Letterach	100	2	1988	10.0
Ladder Hills, Carn Mor	100	2	1988	11.2
Cabrach, Haddoch	100	2	1988	8.0

Cabrach, Tornichelt	50	2	1988	8.0
Ladder Hills, Beinn a' Chruinnich	50	2	1988	12.0
Crathie Burn	200	2	1995	8.0
Rannoch Moor, Ba Cottage	100	1	1996	2.0
Taynuilt, Carn Gaibhre	100	2	2002	2.0

Table 2. Mean spring density (birds per 100 ha), top 13 rows alpine, others moorland. Apart from the last seven rows, where work began in 1973, I chose 1976 for the end of the data used, before any long-term declines became obvious on these areas. For easy reading on the span of years, blank cells have the same values as the first cell above that shows the span.

	Ha	Rock	Span of years	Years	Mean (SE)	Range
Cairngorms, Derry Cairngorm	500	1	1944–76	33	0.5 (0.1)	0–1.2
Cairngorms, Beinn Bhreac	140	1	1945–59	7	2.0 (0.3)	1.4–2.9
Lochnagar, Cac Carn Mor	33	1	1945–76	12	8.1 (0.9)	6.1–12.2
Cairngorms, Moine Bhealaidh	100	2	1946–64	10	9.7 (0.9)	2–14
East Mounth, Glas Maol	107	2	1946–76	23	15.5 (0.9)	9.3–28.0
Cairngorms, Cairn Lochan	220	1	1947–76	29	0.7 (0.1)	0–3.6
Cairngorms, Sron a' Cha-no	150	1		20	2.7 (0.4)	1.3–5.3
Applecross, Bealach na Ba	120	1	1959–61	3	0	0
Durness, Sgribhis Bheinn	100	2		3	21.7 (1.7)	20.0–25.0
Cairngorms, Beinn a' Bhuird	350	1	1968–76	9	2.1 (0.8)	0–6.6
East Mounth, Carn an Tuirc	65	2	1969–70	2	15.4 (3.1)	12.3–18.5
East Mounth, Cairn of Claise	70	2		2	8.5 (2.9)	5.7–11.4
East Mounth, Carn nan Sac	70	2	1969–72	4	15.0 (3.7)	8.6–25.7
Glen Derry	75	1	1944–76	33	9.3 (0.5)	5.3–13.3
Glen Lui	120	1		33	6.8 (0.2)	4.6–9.2
Glen Gairn, Allt Phouple	25	2	1945–71	4	20 (2.3)	16.0–24.0
Abergeldie, Bad a' Chabair	101	1		13	8.1 (1.1)	4.0–13.9
Glen Girnock, Camlet	140	1	1945–75	7	12.7 (0.9)	8.6–15.7
Glen Gairn, Glas-choille	160	2	1946–61	4	10.6 (1.2)	7.5–12.5
Cairn Gorm, Allt Mor	100	1	1946–76	12	2.7 (0.3)	2.0–4.0
Cairn Gorm, Allt na Ciste	75	1		7	6.1 (0.8)	2.7–8.0
Mar Lodge, Creag Bhalg	100	1	1948–76	4	3 (0.6)	2.0–4.0
Spittal of Glenmuick	100	1	1954–58	4	12.0 (1.7)	8.0–16.0
Glen Gairn, The Strone	113	2	1954–76	22	15.4 (1.3)	7.1–28.4

Corndavon, Coulachan	93	2		22	13.5 (1.1)	6.5–25.8
Kerloch V	32	1		18	1.1 (0.6)	0–10
Dunphail, Shian na Youn	58	1	1956–73	6	9.3 (1.2)	5.6–11.2
Dallas, Meikle Hill	53	1		7	11.8 (1.0)	7.5–15.1
Glen Esk low I–VIB	450	2	1957–61	5	12.4 (0.5)	11.1–14.2
Crathie, Monaltrie Moss	300	1		3	7.3 (0.4)	6.7–8.0
Glen Esk V+VIA	59	2	1957–71	15	13.3 (0.8)	7.5–18.9
Sands of Forvie	73	2	1957–73	16	0	-
Crathie Burn, Creag Mhor	100	2	1958–59	2	11.0	10.0–12.0
Glen Esk, Monagob	121	2	1958–61	4	9.2 (1.4)	5.0–11.7
Glen Esk high A–D total	405	2		4	7.0 (1.2)	5.4–10.4
Glen Isla, Craighead	121	2		4	2.9 (0.8)	1.7–5.0
Glen Tarken	121	2		4	0	-
Glen Muick, Craig Vallich	121	2	1958–71	14	3.4 (0.4)	1.7–6.6
Strath Ardle, Dirnanean	84	2	1959–61	3	3.2 (0.8)	2.4–4.8
Glen Dye, Aven	90	1	1960–62	3	11.8 (0.7)	11.1–13.3
Fettercairn, Whitelaws	100	2	1961–76	13	7.2 (0.5)	4–10
Kerloch I	65	1		16	3.8 (0.4)	0–6.2
Kerloch II–IV + XI	327	1		16	8.7 (0.7)	5.5–12.8
Kerloch VI	47	1	1962–76	15	5.1 (0.5)	0–5.9
Kerloch VII	34	1		15	3.7 (0.4)	0–4.3
Kerloch VIII	45	1		15	4.7 (0.3)	4.4–8.8
Kerloch IX	28	1		15	7.6 (0.5)	7.1–14.2
Rickarton, Hill of Allochie	56	2	1964–65	2	3.7 (0)	3.7–3.7
Rickarton, White Hill	42	2		2	4.8 (0)	4.8–4.8
Kerloch X	43	1	1964–76	13	9.8 (0.8)	4.7–18.8
Kerloch XIII	35	1	1965–76	12	6.2 (0.5)	5.7–11.4
Kerloch XIV	36	1		12	5.9 (0.3)	5.6–8.8
Co Mayo, Glenamoy*	310	1	1967–71	5	3.2 (0.9)	1.6–6.5
Pitcarmick Burn	91	2	1968–70	3	4.0 (0.4)	3.3–4.4
Pitcarmick Loch	74	2		3	2.9 (1.7)	0–5.7

Pitcarmick, Dounies west	35	2	1968–72	5	4.3 (1.4)	0–5.7
Pitcarmick, Dounies east	32	2		5	4.7 (1.6)	0–6.3
Atholl, Glen Banvie east	69	1		3	7.6 (2.0)	5.4–11.6
Atholl, Glen Banvie west	54	1		3	11.0 (2.2)	7.2–14.8
Atholl, Glas Choire north	114	1		3	19.6 (0.3)	19.3–20.2
Atholl, Glas Choire south	55	1		3	6.1 (0.6)	5.5–7.3
Pitcarmick, Ballinluig	30	2	1969–71	3	3.3 (3.3)	0–6.7
Pitcarmick, Croft na Coille	30	2		3	3.3 (3.3)	0–6.7
Meikle Corr Riabhach	100	2		3	19.3 (2.4)	16.0–24.0
Dunphail, Bogeney	54	1	1969–73	5	9.0 (1.4)	3.7–7.4
Dunphail, Moidach Mor east	36	1		5	8.0 (1.2)	5.0–10.0
Dunphail, Moidach Mor west	40	1		5	9.0 (1.4)	5.6–11.2
Dallas, Coldburn	66	1		5	7.9 (1.5)	3.0–12.1
Kerloch XV	45	1	1971–76	6	5.1 (0.7)	4.4–8.9
Kerloch XVII	30	1		6	0	-
Kerloch XVIII	10	1		6	0	-
Kerloch XX	11	1	1972–76	5	0	-
Kerloch XIX	20	1	1973–76	4	3.3 (1.1)	0–5.0
Mull, Torloisk, Ensay, A	96	2	1973–84	12	0	-
Mull, Torloisk, Ensay B-C	175	2		12	0.17	0–2.08
Mull, Torloisk, Ensay, D	114	2		12	0.73	0–1.75
Mull, Torloisk, Ensay, E	146	2		6	0	-
Mull, Torloisk, Kilninian F	136	2		6	0	-
Kerloch XXI	37	1	1975–78	4	0	-
Kerloch XXII	28	1		4	0	-

*Glenamoy areas totalled 1000 ha, but only 310 were covered each year. Out of seven areas of blanket bog not used for experiments, no birds were ever seen on two of them. The area with most birds had a mean density of 10.5, range 5–17, highest in 1971. Watson & O'Hare (1979b) give more details.

Table 3. Density (birds per 100 ha) on moorland areas in spring 1957–61.

Place	Area (ha)	1957	1958	1959	1960	1961
Glen Esk low I	65	18.5	9.2	12.3	12.3	15.4
low IIa	49	16.3	16.3	20.4	12.2	16.3
low IIb	57	21.1	17.5	17.5	17.5	17.5
low III	113	10.6	10.6	10.6	10.6	15.9
low IV	53	7.5	3.8	7.5	7.5	7.5
low V & VIA	59	10.2	13.6	10.2	13.6	16.9
low VIB	65	6.2	6.2	9.2	6.2	6.2
low I–VIB, total	450	12.4	11.1	12.4	11.6	14.2
low VII	43	-	-	-	4.7	4.7
high A	121	8.3	6.6	11.6	5.0	6.6
high B	121	-	8.3	14.9	6.6	6.6
high C	121	-	5.0	6.6	5.0	5.0
high D	42	-	4.8	4.8	4.8	4.8
high A–D, total	405	-	6.4	10.4	5.4	5.9
Glen Esk, Gairney	105	-	-	3.8	1.9	3.8
Glen Esk, Braid Cairn	194	-	1.1	2.2	2.2	2.2
Glen Esk, Punchbowl	121	-	5.0	9.9	9.9	11.6
Angus, Glen Isla	121	-	1.7	3.3	1.7	5.0
Loch Earn, Glen Tarken	121	-	0	0	0	0
Sands of Forvie	73	-	0	0	0	0
Glen Muick, Craig Vallich	121	-	3.3	3.3	1.7	5
Corndavon, Coulachan	93	10.7	8.6	12.9	9.7	17.2
Corndavon, Creag Mhor	100	-	0	0	-	-
Abergeldie, Bad a' Chabair	101	-	-	-	-	9.9
Strath Ardle, Dirnanean	84	-	-	2.4	2.4	4.8
Glen Derry	75	10.7	8.0	10.7	10.7	13.3
Glen Lui	130	6.2	4.6	7.7	7.7	9.2

Table 4. Positive correlation coefficients (r) between spring numbers on moorland study areas in the four years 1958–61. First value is coefficient, last value P (not shown where > 0.2). Glen Esk high was on high moorland, others on lower moorland.

	Corndavon	Glen Isla	Glen Esk low	Glen Esk high
Glen Isla	0.993, 0.007			
Glen Esk low	0.996, 0.004	0.984, 0.016		
Glen Esk high	0.117, 0.88	0.171, 0.83	0.03, 0.97	
Punchbowl	0.949, 0.08	0.833, 0.08	0.949, 0.08	−0.316, 0.75
Glen Muick	0.633, 0.33	0.861, 0.18	0.633, 0.33	0.316, 0.75

Density at Glen Esk high area was poorly associated with that on other areas, including the nearby Glen Esk low area.

Table 5. Positive correlation coefficients (r_s) between spring numbers in the 11 years 1961–71, P value after comma.

	Glen Derry	Glen Lui	Corndavon	Glen Esk*	Abergeldie
Glen Lui	0.880, 0.0004				
Corndavon	0.753, 0.009	0.545, 0.082			
Glen Esk*	0.822, 0.003	0.822, 0.003	0.661, 0.031		
Abergeldie^	0.820, 0.003	0.651, 0.034	0.750, 0.010	0.700, 0.019	
Glen Muick	0.787, 0.006	0.787, 0.006	0.568, 0.071	0.847, 0.0016	0.854, 0.0013

* Parts V+VIA of the Low area.

^ Bad a' Chabair.

Table 6. Correlation coefficients (r_s) between spring numbers on three alpine areas. First value shows coefficient, second in parentheses is number of years, and the third is the P value (not shown where >0.2). Data are up to 1987 inclusive, before long-term declines had occurred on alpine areas.

	Cairn Lochan	Beinn a' Bhuird	Derry Cairngorm
Beinn a' Bhuird	0.621 (20), 0.0041		
Derry Cairngorm	0.638 (43), <0.0001	0.705 (20), 0.0007	
Glas Maol	–0.069 (35)	–0.093 (20)	0.144 (35)

Table 7. Proportionate change in number of golden plover from spring $i-1$ to spring i on Glas Maol in relation to breeding success in summer $i-1$ (first row of data), and (other rows) on Glas Maol and elsewhere in relation to the number in spring $i-1$, and (footnote) to breeding success on Glas Maol in summer i in relation to the number in spring i. Data at Glas Maol are up to 1987 inclusive, before long-term decline occurred there, elsewhere up to 1976 as in Table 2.

Proportionate change in relation to	n of years	Coefficient (r_s)	P
breeding success in summer $i-1$ at Glas Maol	26	0.482	0.0135
number of adults in spring $i-1$ at			
Glen Derry	33	–0.624	0.0001
Glen Lui	33	–0.722	<0.0001
Glas Maol	33	–0.648	0
Corndavon, Coulachan Burn	21	–0.569	0.008
Kerloch II–IV+XI	16	–0.353	0.18
Glen Esk low V+VIA	14	–0.691	0.0078
Glen Muick, Craig Vallich	13	–0.679	0.0129
Abergeldie, Bad a' Chabair	11	–0.460	0.15
Glenamoy	4	–0.800	0.33
Glen Esk high A	4	–0.800	0.33
Dunphail, Moidach Mor west	4	–0.707	0.33

Breeding success at Glas Maol in summer i was correlated negatively with adult numbers in spring i ($n = 27$ years, $r_s = -0.411$, $P = 0.034$). Data on breeding elsewhere too fragmentary for analysis.

Table 8. Change in spring number at Glas Maol since previous spring, in relation to mean air temperature in January, February and March of current spring at Leuchars, and number of days of air frost at Leuchars in January, February and October–April, in 31 years up to 1987 before long-term declines began. For 14 years at Glen Esk low area A in 1957–71, $r = 0.545$ and 0.353 for January and February air temperatures at Leuchars, $P = 0.044$ and 0.215.

	r	P
January temperature	0.261	0.16
February temperature	0.469	0.0078
January days of air frost	−0.592	0.026
February days of air frost	−0.360	0.21
October–April days of air frost	−0.558	0.038

Table 9. Mean density (birds per 100 ha) in spring 1958–61 on 15 moorland study areas in north-east Scotland in relation to a) the mean height of heather (cm) in autumn 1959 and b) a score for its mean age as assessed in each spring and autumn during 1959–61 and c) the proportion of the ground covered by heather (Miller *et al.* 1966).

	n of areas	r	P
Height	18	−0.750	0.0003
Age	17	−0.706	0.0015
Cover	17	−0.1	0.7

Table 10. Correlation coefficients on the lowest parts of the Kerloch study area, between the number of birds during spring and the calendar year, up to 1976 inclusive. All parts were heavily grazed when the study began in 1961, with much short heather.

Area	Fencing	r_s	P
I	fenced	−0.804	0.0002
V	fenced	−0.420	0.11
II+III+IV+XI	unfenced	0.765	0.0008

Parts I and V were fenced in autumn 1961 to exclude sheep and cattle for years up to autumn 1977, and during these years the vegetation grew taller. Meanwhile the other parts stayed open to heavy grazing. Part XI had no grazing during a few summers in the 1960s, when the farmer grew oats and turnips on the adjacent unfenced field. The heather was burned in rotational strip fires from spring 1962 onwards on part I and the upper sections of parts II and IV, but not on V. Heavy grazing on the lower sections of II and

IV, and all of III and XI, kept heather too short for burning to be needed for grouse management. No burning was done on part V, to allow for experiments where fertiliser was applied to heather. In the first year after fencing, golden plover became extinct on part V, which had only small flushes. On part I with two large wide flushes, they declined from two pairs in 1961–65 to one pair in 1966–75 and then to none in 1976. After the farmer opened the gate to part I in 1978 and allowed cattle and sheep to graze, a pair was present in 1979–82, rising to two pairs in 1983–87 although numbers fell on other parts of the area. By 1988 they had become extinct again on part I and everywhere by 1989 (Parr 1992b).

Appendix. Habitat features associated with presence and abundance

Table 3 shows a negative relationship between the density of golden plover and the mean height of heather, but does not identify a preferred height. To find this would require a study of habitat usage. A useful clue is that Parr (1990) found the mean height of vegetation at 56 nests on moorland to be 9.38 cm (SE 0.51). Some nests on territories used for a number of years by the same birds were in taller heather of 15 cm, but all newly established birds nested in short vegetation (mean 4.4 cm).

On moorland, vegetation height can change within a few years owing to burning or grazing. On alpine land, vegetation is permanently short because of slow growth, exposure, and die-back. As expected from the above relationship between plover density and heather height, plover densities on some alpine land were high. They exceeded any densities recorded on north-east Scottish moorland.

Other factors are involved besides vegetation height. Mean densities of golden plover on Glas Maol and nearby hills in the Mounth hill-range exceeded those at similar altitudes on the Cairngorms. An obvious difference is that acidic granite forms most bedrock in the Cairngorms, whereas base-rich schists predominate on the Mounth. Soils derived from the granite are mostly coarse and incohesive, with thin infertile topsoil, associated with a high proportion of bare ground. On the schist, for example on Glas Maol, they have thicker and more fertile topsoil, supporting a complete vegetation cover except on a few screes and exposed ridges.

Densities of golden plover were very low on study areas in the western part of the Isle of Mull, and almost as low on wet Irish blanket bog at Glenamoy in north Co Mayo. Ground in both locations is generally wet and precipitation heavy. The thick peat results in acidic infertile conditions, where soil invertebrates are scarce and earthworms absent.

Golden plover are well known to avoid steep slopes. Sub-areas XV and XVII–XXVII at Kerloch, mapped in Moss *et al.* (2000) had slopes of 15–28 degrees, and no golden plover was seen there in 1961–78 except on the few flattish parts. Kerloch sub-areas with breeding birds had gradients of 0–12 degrees. Elsewhere I saw none on gradients >15 degrees on upper parts of Glen Muick study area, the main slope of Braid Cairn, most of part D on high Glen Esk, the steep part of VI at low Glen Esk, steep slopes around plateaux on Glas Maol, Cairn Lochan, Beinn a' Bhuird and Carn nan Sac, study areas at Meall Odhar and Cairnwell (20 ha each), and steep sub-alpine moorland at Cairnwell (13 ha) and Sunnyside (14 ha). The only birds seen on the Derry Cairngorm area were on the sole flattish tracts, the slopes that form almost all of the area being avoided.

Birds avoided lightly grazed groundwater flushes with perennially flowing surface water, where bog myrtle and rushes grew tall, a habitat favoured by snipe. Golden plover used such flushes for foraging with chicks if flushes were heavily grazed, as on part II at low Glen Esk. Birds with chicks at low Glen Esk also favoured small flushes where surface water flowed only after heavy rain, as on section VIA. Broods on moorland also used patches of short, heavily grazed bent-fescue grassland (*Agrostis capillaris* and *Festuca ovina*), as at Kerloch (Parr 1990).

Chapter 5. Decline of breeding golden plover since 1970

Summary

Breeding golden plover (*Pluvialis apricaria*) have declined greatly on moorland and alpine land in north-east Scotland, at some areas down to nil. The numbers in flocks feeding in nearby fields have also fallen. The main decline occurred in the late 1970s and in the 1980s, but on a few areas has continued since 1988. Extinction on a few areas followed destruction of moorland habitat by tree-planting or colonisation by scrub and natural tree regeneration, or by grass reseeding, or by heather becoming too tall after grazing by farm stock or burning ceased. On most areas, these changes in land management did not occur.

Most declines and extinctions occurred before 1988, and hence before recent increases of gulls, crows and ravens (*Corvus corax*) as potential predators, and before recent climatic warming in north-east Scotland. These last two possible factors can therefore be discounted as possible causes of the main early declines before 1988, though they may be involved in the later declines. Predation on eggs and chicks by ravens might have contributed to later declines, e.g. Whitfield (2002) attributed a decline of dotterel at East Drumochter to ravens taking eggs.

I suggest that intensification of agriculture on the bird's wintering grounds near the east coast, especially a massive decline of permanent pasture, is a sufficient condition for most declines. Such intensification is not a necessary condition, as shown by localised extirpations following the above-mentioned habitat loss or deterioration.

Introduction

Declines to local extirpation in recent decades have been documented for breeding golden plover on two moorland study areas in north-east Scotland, at Kerloch near Banchory in Kincardineshire (Parr 1992) and near Tarfside at Glen Esk in Angus (Jenkins & Watson 2001). In the present paper I report declines on many other moorland and alpine areas. In no case has there been an increase or no change. The period covered is 1944–2012. I review the above two published declines, and other published information. This indicates that declines are general.

Study areas

Most areas were chosen for research on red grouse (*Lagopus lagopus scoticus*) on moorland and ptarmigan (*Lagopus mutus*) on alpine land, but a few for work on the food potential of golden eagles (*Aquila chrysaetos*) and on dunlin (*Calidris alpina*). Study areas for these purposes have been described elsewhere, including maps (Jenkins *et al.* 1963, 1967; Brown & Watson 1964; Watson 1965, 1979; Watson *et al.* 1989, 1998; Parr 1990; Rae & Watson 1998). I used a few other areas incidentally in the course of other work.

Methods

These involved counting settled pairs in spring and in the breeding season by counts based on scanning with binoculars, searching with pointing dogs, and locating singing cocks at the dawn or dusk chorus. They have been described and validated elsewhere (Watson & O'Hare 1979; Parr 1990, 1992a and b).

The timing of observations spanned from mid February till mid September, but the data on pairs rested on counts in April–May. Adults and fledged young gathered in flocks during late June-early August on moorland, and mid July to late August on alpine land. Some adults that had failed to rear young left the areas earlier than those with young. This happened especially on moorland, though on alpine land they more often stayed. Birds with late-hatched young also stayed, up to late August on moorland and early September on alpine land, and in the case of moorland after all other birds had gone.

Flocks on alpine land in August and later may have included immigrants that did not breed on the area, and in some years were so large that they must have comprised mostly immigrants, e.g. 100+ on Cairn Lochan in October 1988 (Dennis 1995). Nonetheless, they provided a useful index of change, albeit not confined to a particular study area.

Results on moorland areas with habitat loss or deterioration

A book by AW & Ian Francis on *Birds in north-east Scotland then and now* (2012) describes many places where I found breeding golden plover in the 1940s but where they have since long become extinct. The observations were quantitative but did not involve counts on defined areas. Many of these areas lay in northern Aberdeenshire and the northern parts of the then Banffshire, and another set of areas in mid Deeside from Drumnagesk east of Aboyne to Muir of Dinnet and Ordie Moss. In at least one case the birds colonised an area after clear-felling of woodland for the war effort. In some cases, dense planting of coniferous trees destroyed the moorland. In many cases, cessation of grazing by farm stock and of muirburn led to tall rank heather becoming unsuitable for the birds, along with invasion by scrub and trees. At Muir of Dinnet this led to large-scale expansion of natural woodland. The scrub and trees also dried the ground by removing more water from the soil.

Tilquhillie

On this small moor I found one pair in 1963 and 1964 on a 120-ha section, where they bred, and I heard birds calling on other parts of the moor. Birds summered annually thereafter. However, Economic Forestry Group planted the whole moor with conifers in the 1980s, using taxpayers' grants. This destroyed the moorland.

Rickarton

On this moor near the coast, I found two pairs in April 1964 during a count of red grouse with pointing dogs on a 120-ha section at the eastern end, one of them on Hill of Allochie and one on the more isolated White Hill. They bred there. Cattle and sheep grazed the moor lightly, and it had been burned rotationally, so there was much short heather and no tall degenerate heather.

In 1979–89 the whole moor including Hill of Allochie and White Hill formed a study area for research on red grouse, and counts were done regularly every spring and August, as well as many searches in April–July for grouse nests and chicks. We saw no golden plover on Hill of Allochie, the White Hill, and other nearby sections.

Sheep still grazed the hill lightly, but there had been very little muirburn since the mid 1960s, so most of the heather had grown tall and dense, with no young heather on Hill of Allochie or White Hill. Although we then burned a substantial proportion of the moor, and young heather regenerated well, we continued to see no golden plover, and found none breeding anywhere on the 1021 ha of moorland in the 11 years of study. A pair was seen on an April day on the top of Craigneil in 1989, resting on a large patch that had been burned, but not next day or thereafter. I found none on Hill of Allochie and White Hill in spring 1990–2011.

Kerloch
Parr (1992, 1993) did a detailed study on the lower part of this moor as described in more detail in the next main section below. Numbers were high for many years but declined sharply in the late 1970s and became extinct by 1990. Most birds bred on the lower parts of the moor where Parr studied them, but a few on blanket bog or thick peat higher up. Fountain Forestry destroyed most of that upper moorland by dense tree-planting in the early 1980s. In 1961 I did a few counts of red grouse on that upper area, and again a few later years, and noted any golden plover seen. I estimate that on average the moorland that was destroyed used to hold about eight breeding pairs.

Results on moorland without habitat loss or deterioration
Glen Esk
At a large study area ('the Low area') on moorland beside farm fields near Tarfside, many occurred each year in 1957–61, varying from 25 pairs after a cold snowy winter in 1958 to 32 pairs in 1961 after a mild winter, and with a mean density of 6.2 pairs per 100 ha (Jenkins & Watson 2001). The area held none in 1988–98 (Jenkins & Watson 2001) and 1999–2012, a significant decline with the year (Table 1).

In May to June 1957–61, flocks commonly fed on grass fields within the Low area during March–June, and sometimes later. There were many fields, and usually small flocks of 4–10 birds occurred in any one field, with annual numbers typically totalling 30–120 on all fields combined on any one day. Sometimes a flock held more, such as 20 in a grass field at Baillies on 7 May 1958. The most favoured fields, at the Baillies farm and at abandoned former arable farms at Arsallary, had permanent pasture. I saw no flocks totalling more than 10 birds on the 7-year rotational arable fields at Milton inside the study area. This, however, was confounded by the fact that permanent grass pasture lay next to the largest block of continuous moorland.

I observed birds flying to the fields from higher ground and from moorland surrounding the Low area. In every summer, including dry summers such as 1959, flocks occurred on the fields into early July, e.g. David Jenkins saw 19 in a field on 1 July 1957, and in 1959 found 35 on a nearby grassy part of the moor on 5 July and 20 on 9 July. In the wet summer of 1958, when earthworms still abounded on grass fields through late July and into August, flocks still fed there, e.g. David Jenkins noted 'large flocks' on grass fields at Baillies farm on 8 August and I counted about 130 there on 10 August.

Small flocks fed on grass fields elsewhere

in Glen Esk, at Auchronie, Dalbrack, Migvie, Keenie, Blackcraigs and Mill of Aucheen, e.g. 12 at the latter place on 2 May 1958. During annual visits in April–June 1988–2011 I found none at these places or at the above others in Glen Esk, but I did not visit the formerly best fields, at Baillies, in years after 1999.

In June 2011, Alan Finlayson, who has lived for long with his family at Burnside on our Low study area, told me that it was many years since he saw any golden plover in the fields there or further down the study area at Whitestone, Milton Cottage and Milton, and likewise years since he heard or saw any on the moorland nearby (our old study areas I, II, III, IV, V and VI).

However, gamekeeper Kevin, who lives with his family at Milton, told Alan Finlayson and me on 10 April 2012 that a flock of about 30 were that day in the grass field beside a large sandy hillock at the Baillies, and had been there daily for several weeks during the March heatwave. He added that the nearest place where he had found breeding birds in late spring and summer, including 2011, was on Pullar Cuy, a peaty hill reaching 636 m and rising above the upper Water of Tarf.

Morven Lodge

On 10 April 1944 I saw four pairs by the roadside while cycling for 2.3 km on a road across moorland from Lary to Morven Lodge, on a 1.1 km flat section southwards from the grass fields at the Lodge. They were settled, displaying and calling loudly. Two more pairs fed in a grass field near the shepherd's house above the lodge. I saw similar numbers in a number of other years up to 1976, from 3–5 pairs. In May 1995 when I walked the same route, I observed none near the road or in the fields. Gamekeeper James Scott walked at the same time across the boggy moor parallel to the road and 500 m from it, with a pointer ranging, and saw and heard no plover. I heard a distant pair calling on higher ground. In annual visits during May since then, up to 2012, I have seen or heard none while walking up and down the glen.

Glas-choille

At this side glen in upper Glen Gairn, two pairs had chicks near the roadside in 1946 and often fed on the grassy verge in April and May, while a third pair bred in the bog below the bridge. I saw similar numbers in a few years up to 1961. They fed mostly on abandoned grass fields at Glenfenzie farm. Other pairs bred in bogs west of Allt Glas-choille, and on high ground on either side of the glen. In April 1981 I saw 12 pairs on the bogs of Moine Allt Duisgan north of the farm, plus a flock of 10 at the farm. In May 1993, Robert Rae and I heard none on the whole Glas-choille basin during dusk observations, although birds still called from high ground at Carn a' Bhacain and Scraulac on either side. I found none in the glen during annual visits in May 1994–2012. Robert Moss told me that during many counts of red grouse on the Glas-choille basin in the late 1990s and early 2000s, he and colleagues saw no golden plover there, though they heard birds calling on high ground to the west.

Corndavon

In spring 1954–71, several pairs nested annually on a 93-ha study area on Corndavon moor, reaching a peak of 12 pairs in 1971. One pair was there annually in 1986–89 (Parr 1993), but I found none in 1990–2011.

Small flocks fed in April–June on nearby grass fields at the abandoned farm of Bad Fiantaige north of Coulachan Burn, and on arable fields at Blairglass farm and Cnoc Chalmac. On 13 April 1958, for example, 27 fed at the Coulachan fields, and on 17 April 1973 there were 17 in a field at Cnoc Chalmac and 25 at Blairglass. Birds still came to feed in permanent pasture fields after Blairglass farmer Willie Findlay stopped arable farming about 1973, for instance in 1981, and on 26 March 1982 I saw 11 there, but none in annual spring visits during 1999–2012.

On the nearby Monaltrie Moss there were 32, 30 and 36 pairs in 1957, 1965 and 1971, but only 12 pairs in 1988. Robert Rae and I found six pairs with nests or young during May and early June 1997, and I saw the same number in 1998. Mick Marquiss told me that he with R. Rae saw none in early summer 2006.

Abergeldie

Flocks annually fed on fields at Buailteach above Lochnagar Distillery, at their largest when snow covered the moor. In the late afternoon of 25 April 1970, when deep snow blanketed ground above 800 m and lay at 1–5 cm depth down to 600 m altitude, I counted 320 on these fields. During the 1960s and 1970s there were usually about 20 during the middle part of the day, rising to 30–40 in evenings and early mornings. On 6 May 1986 only two birds arrived to feed, and on 24 May none. On 29 April 1987, 6 June 1987 and 14 April 1988 I again saw none, and annually none in 1989–2012. Nearby resident John Robertson saw none there since 1990 during frequent annual trips motoring up the private road.

In 1958–69, resident gamekeeper Charles Wright found them abundant on peat mosses in Glen Girnock, especially at Coire na Cloiche including the lower moss Moine na Cloiche, with the highest density further up where the ground was wetter. Numbers began to fall there in 1967–69.

A flock on grass fields at Bovaglie farm numbered 20–30 in the 1940s–70s, with up to 100 when fresh snowfalls covered the moor. Numbers declined greatly in the 1980s, down to 6–10 by 1987 and fewer by 1989 (told to me by ranger Neil Cook). Abergeldie estate destroyed the site in the 1990s by planting trees on the fields, using Forestry Commission grants.

On a 101-ha moorland area in upper Glen Girnock, used for studies of red grouse in 1961–71, I found golden plover breeding annually in 1945–49, 1954–57, and 1961–71. Parr (1993) saw a pair in 1986 and 1987, but none in 1988 or 1989. In June 2002, however, Rodney Heslop, John Robertson, Alexander Walker and I saw a pair with at least two chicks a week old, at the roadside south of the bridge. Further south in June 2008 we saw a pair flying around us and giving alarm calls, obviously with chicks nearby in a flush, and likewise a second pair west of the 101-ha area but close to it. J. Robertson and I found none in June 2010 or in 2011.

Lower Glen Clunie

Small flocks up to a total of about 25 birds foraged on grazed grass fields between Braemar and Auchallater each April-May in 1946–79, e.g. 22 in a field just south of Braemar on 13 May 1973. I saw none there during annual visits in 1980–2012.

Glen Lui

In 1944–81, 4–5 pairs bred annually on the

boggy floor, and often fed on permanent pasture at abandoned former arable farms. I saw none there annually since 1982, and none was found during a survey in 1998 (Mountains to Marine 1999).

Glen Derry

In July 1945, three pairs had large young at the lochan, and in other years in 1944–81 there were usually 1–2 pairs there, and another pair nearby on the upper grassy flats. I saw none annually in 1982–2012, and the 1998 survey (above) revealed none.

Glen Muick

At Spittal of Glenmuick in 1930–80, J. Robertson and his father were used to seeing a flock of 20–30 feeding in spring on grass fields grazed by sheep and on ploughed arable fields nearby, and up to 100 came when fresh snow covered the hills. Numbers dwindled in the early 1980s, down to none in 1984–87 and none annually since.

In the late 1940s to late 1970s, John Robertson found on average about 20 pairs on peat mosses at the Black Burn above Loch Muick (5.5 square km), and 10–12 on 6 square km on the Glen Mark side of Fasheilach and the Black Hill of Mark. He estimated that there would have been hundreds of birds on the peaty hills between Loch Muick and the upper parts of Glen Esk and Glen Clova. When searching for foxes at night, he found that the plovers' calls gave him a continuous location for a fox crossing areas where different birds had nests or young. He also saw pairs throughout the wide boggy bottom of Glen Muick, though at lower density.

On the Black Burn and other peaty ground nearby, breeding numbers plunged at the end of the 1970s and early 1980s. He noticed far fewer returning in spring after cold snowy winters, especially after the winter of 1981–82 which was especially severe in Angus and Glen Muick.

Feindallacher Burn

In 1970–79, C. Wright saw a few pairs breeding every year on peaty moorland around the upper Feindallacher Burn, and on boggy patches of alpine land on the White Mounth, but they became scarcer by 1980 and fell in numbers further during the early 1980s.

White Hill at Forest of Birse on upper Feugh

Prior to 1980, they bred annually and commonly on moorland such as White Hill, Cock Hill, Gannoch, Tampie and Hill of Duchery. Often they fed in flocks on grazed grass fields at Ballochan farm, but not after the early 1980s (D. Jenkins, as told by gamekeepers R. Fraser, Leslie George and Robbie Paterson, and DJ's annual observations at the fields in 1987–2007). I saw one foraging briefly in a grass field there on the evening of 3 May 2007, but none in May 2008 or in spring annually since then. David Jenkins told me in April 2012 that in late spring 2011 he accompanied gamekeeper Robbie Paterson in his vehicle on to the high ground towards Gannoch, west of the Fungle track. Paterson pointed out a pair and said this was the only pair that he knew still nesting on the estate.

Kerloch

Many bred in 1961–70 on moorland used for intensive studies of red grouse, and flocks fed in grass fields nearby. Parr (1992, 1993) did a detailed study using colour-ringed birds, finding >100 breeding in the early-mid 1970s. They wintered on farmland near the Angus coast south-west of Montrose. Few marked birds returned to Kerloch in spring after severe winters on Angus lowland in 1977–79 and 1981–84, and the population became extinct by 1990. I have seen none on annual visits in March–July since.

Corgarff
Many golden plover have long bred on peaty high moorland along the Ladder Hills north of the River Don near Corgarff in Strathdon, Aberdeenshire, and along Brown Cow Hill and other hills south of Don. Smooth short grassland is very scarce on the thick peat, and for decades the birds have flown in flocks to arable and pasture fields on farms in the glens on either side of the Ladder Hills and the hill-range to the south. In 1981–85 I saw up to four birds at a time on early mornings in summer, foraging on re-seeded short grass beside the public road from Cock Bridge to Tomintoul, just south of its highest point.

They regularly came in larger numbers to the fields at lower altitude, from April till June. Flocks on the fields increased during the early morning and especially the late evening, irrespective of weather, but reached maximum size on evenings when fresh snow lay on the nesting grounds. On 13 May 1968, when deep snow lay on surrounding hilltops, 80 foraged on short grass at a reseeded area above Allargue, which was only thinly covered with snow. On 11 April 1969 my father saw a flock of 250 there. This reseeded ground has seldom been used by the birds in the 1990s and 2000s, when the grass became taller and rougher due to less grazing by sheep.

On snow-free grass fields along the main road at Corgarff I noted 'many hundreds' during evenings in May 1968, when deep fresh snow covered the hills for weeks. This included 120 on fields at Dykehead. The Dykehead fields usually had a flock of about 60–70 birds when the hills were not snow-covered, and when deep snow covered the hills the flock was about this size throughout the day. Numbers fell during the 1980s. On 28 April 1996, the flock in fields by the main road at Dykehead numbered only seven birds, and numbers declined further in the late 1990s. I saw none on the evening of 8 May 2007 there or on other fields along the main road. On the evening of 11 May 2007 a single cock foraged in the most favoured field west of Dykehead, but in April–May 2007 and annually since, none except 7 in 2012.

Other favoured fields were at Corgarff Castle, receiving birds from Brown Cow Hill and Camock Hill, and on an evening in early May 1983 I saw 160 arriving in flocks of 20–40 at a time, and in the most favoured field west of Corgarff Castle I watched an additional two cocks (one singing as he landed) beside a hen.

Gamekeeper David Scrimgeour has lived for many years near the Castle, working at Delnadamph moor on the south side of Don, which includes the north side of Brown Cow Hill. He has also managed the fields at the Castle. In 2007 he told me that there had been a big decline of golden plover coming to fields at Dykehead and the Castle, and since 2003 he has seen far fewer on their breeding grounds on the hill. At the Castle fields he was used to seeing flocks of 50–100 and totalling about 120 in the 1990s, but in the next few years the flocks totalled a few tens of birds at most. In two or three late springs, snow fell in April and May on the breeding grounds, and he saw unusually large numbers in the flocks into May and June, which he thought may have swollen by birds which had deserted their nests or whose chicks had died. Numbers in subsequent years reached a trough about 2004. They picked up to some extent in 2005 on the fields and on the hill, but in 2006 were the scarcest he had ever seen there. In the fields during late April 2007 he saw 15, in 2008 a flock of about 20, and in 2011 up to 30.

Edinglassie of Don

To the east of Corgarff lies Edinglassie moor on the north side of Don, stretching to the top of the Ladder Hills. Head-keeper Derek Calder told me in 2007 that for many years the birds had flocked in spring to feed in old grass fields on abandoned farms at Relaqheim, Lynardoch and Bressachoil, and off-duty birds during the incubation period also visited the fields throughout daylight hours. In the late 1980s the flocks totalled about 60 birds, but then declined, until in recent years there have been only 20 or fewer. The number seen on the moor during the breeding season has fallen in like proportion. He was concerned that they might become locally extinct. However, in 2011 he found a substantial increase on the lower moorland, where birds nested on patches of burnt heather in places not used for some years. They had bred well during an unusually wet June and July, and he and the under-keepers saw many big young in the first two weeks of July. Numbers on the higher hills had not changed noticeably in his view, and likewise the numbers coming to the fields.

Results on alpine and sub-alpine land

Glas Maol

On the alpine plateau of upper Glas Maol, spring numbers showed no material change until a marked decline in 1987–88, and even lower numbers more recently (Table 1). Numbers in flocks during August–early September have also declined. On 6 August 1946, Bernard W. Tucker and I found a flock of 100, and I have never seen so many since. Except for a flock of 62 in 2007, in the 10 years 2003–12 I saw none in August.

Meall Odhar near Glas Maol

During each breeding season in 1964–85, a pair was at the bog south-east of the col and another at flushes north-east of Meall Odhar, but I found only the latter site occupied in 1986 and 1987, and not in 1988–2012. Two pairs bred on the upper part of a 20-ha study area for ptarmigan on the west side of Meall Odhar in 1963 and 1964, one pair annually until 1970 inclusive and again in 1977, 2010 and 2012, but none during other years in 1971–2011.

On 6 August 1946, B.W. Tucker and I saw a flock of 40 on alpine land at the col between Meall Odhar and Glas Maol, but in Augusts after 1964 a flock of only 10 or fewer was there in some years, and I saw none in 1981–2012.

Other land near Glenshee Ski Centre

In 1963–70 I found a pair annually in each of the four following places on sub-alpine land, the bog below Butchart's Corrie north of the Cairnwell, the top of Meall Odhar Beag, the slope south of the top, and the corrie north-east of the top.. The site south of Meall Odhar Beag was still occupied until summer 1978, when birds reared young, and in 1978 a pair nested at a site not used in 1964–77, east of the main car park at Glenshee ski centre. A pair nested at a peaty, heather-dominated shallow slope on alpine land along the upper part of the Cairnwell in 1978 and 1979, but I saw none there in 1963–77 or 1980 onwards, and in 1988–2012 none at any of these sites.

Many occurred in flocks during late summer and early autumn on or near Carn nan Sac, and also on Carn an Tuirc north-east of Glenshee Ski Centre. For example, there was a flock of 150 between Carn nan Sac and Loch Vrotachan on 8 August 1964, but in 1988 and since I have seen only small flocks, up to 20, and on 8 September 2004 none on or near Carn nan Sac. On 10 September 2004 the flock on Carn an Tuirc numbered only 24.

Alpine land on the Cairngorms massif
Beinn a' Bhuird is in the eastern Cairngorms north of Braemar and Cairn Lochan south-west of Cairn Gorm. The number of birds in spring declined with the year on both areas (Table 1).

On Derry Cairngorm, a study area for ptarmigan held a pair of golden plover, recorded by Watson (1965), and a pair annually in 1946–82. They frequented a flush south of Little Cairngorm. Two extra pairs bred in 1960, 1961 and 1969, one in a peat bog further down the same flush, and one at a flush south-west of Derry Cairngorm summit, and in 1969 a fourth pair at a flush east of Little Cairngorm. In 1960 and 1961 a pair nested at a flush outside the study area, north-east of the summit. I saw none in 1987–99, and none was found during the 1998 survey (above).

In 1947–65, the boggy alpine grasslands of Monadh Mor held 1–2 pairs on the Geusachan (Aberdeenshire) side, and 1–2 pairs on the Eidart (Inverness-shire) side. In 1946–65, 2–3 pairs occurred on boggy grasslands north and north-west of the Devil's Point, towards Cairn Toul. During the 1998 survey (above), no birds were found on the Aberdeenshire side of Monadh Mor and Cairn Toul.

The peaty grassy alpine plateau of Moine Bhealaidh held quite a high density of breeding birds in 1946–64. Only one pair was found during the 1998 survey (above) and likewise in two other years with observations since 1990.

Discussion
Declines or extinctions on study areas with habitat loss or deterioration
On Tilquhillie moor, extinction coincided with habitat loss from conversion of moorland to woodland by tree-planting, and this occurred on a few sections at Kerloch along with colonisation by natural tree regeneration and scrub. On a few other areas that remained as moorland, such as Rickarton and two sections at Kerloch that were fenced, extinction coincided with habitat deterioration where heather grew tall as a result of sheep and cattle being fenced out, along with less burning or no burning. However, these events did not apply on most moorland areas and also on all alpine areas.

Other declines recorded
An early report of a decline came from Dorback moor in Strathspey (Nethersole-Thompson & Watson 1974). Nethersole-Thompson found at least 25–30 pairs in the late 1930s and early 1940s, but they

declined in the 1950s, and by the late 1960s had decreased to less than half the original number. In 1952 he found 15–20 pairs (Nethersole-Thompson 1952). Dennis (1995) noted 'very few now'.

Declines have been recorded in Moray and Nairn. Surveys on two big moorland areas revealed 33 pairs in 1980, falling to 12 pairs in 1989 (references in Cook 1992).

Extinction at Kerloch

It is instructive to concentrate on this case, because it was the most intensive population study yet done on golden plover in the UK. The decline on Kerloch moor coincided with a low rate of return of birds in spring from the wintering grounds on coastal Scottish farmland after snowy frosty winters (Parr 1992b). Also there has been a loss of permanent pasture on lowland, including the wintering grounds for Parr's birds near the Angus coast. Large flocks wintering in north-east Scotland have favoured such pasture for decades. It has been replaced mostly by autumn-sown crops of cereal and oilseed rape, and to a lesser extent other short-term crops.

Breeding success became very poor only in the later years of the decline, due to egg-robbing by predators, which increased in 1982 following the start of tree-planting in 1981 and an end to game-keeping. After re-analysing Parr's data, Harding *et al.* (1994) decided that nest predation accounted better for the decline. This was erroneous. Parr's data show that breeding success did not fall until 1982, yet the decline in the total number of birds began in 1977–78, continued until 1979, and remained low until spring 1982. The decline in the number of territories occupied on the main study area decreased in 1975–77, remained low in 1978, 1981 and 1982 (no data in 1979 and 1980), and rose up to 1984 before falling sharply down to 1985. Poor breeding may have prevented a recovery (Parr 1992b, 1993). The most one can argue for predation is that it may have maintained a decline which began for a different reason.

Gibbons *et al.* (2007) repeated the argument of Harding *et al.*, stating that although the decline could have been explained by high losses of adults during winter, the evidence suggested that it was most likely a consequence of nest predation. Further, they stated incorrectly that the decline 'coincided with the cessation of predator control and the planting of conifers close to the breeding area'. Neither the cessation nor the planting occurred until years after the decline began.

The argument of Gibbons *et al.* about cessation of game-keeping and planting of conifers is rejected by events on the Low area at Glen Esk. Jenkins & Watson (2001) documented that golden plover occurred at high density there in 1957–61, but none was found in the late 1980s and 1990s. This area and land for miles around had no tree-planting on moorland and no change in the number and activities of gamekeepers. Therefore this case rejects the generality of the arguments of Harding *et al.* and Gibbons *et al.* about golden plover.

Many other cases on moorland and alpine land as documented in Table 1 and the above text also reject their arguments. There has been no change in the number of gamekeepers on estates owning these areas, and no loss of moorland by tree-planting.

Predation and climatic warming as possible causes of declines

Since the mid 1980s, ravens have become all-season resident foragers on study areas in the east Mounth such as Glas Maol, and have been found to take eggs of golden plover, ptarmigan and dotterel, and probably take chicks also. Likewise, common gulls (*Larus canus*) rob eggs of golden plover (Parr 1993), and I have seen common gulls take chicks of other species and feed them to young gulls. Common gulls too have increased as breeders in or near many study areas, including Glas Maol and nearby hills. Hence one possibility is that predation on eggs or chicks caused the decline of golden plover at Glas Maol. This can be rejected, because breeding success did not fall in 1987 prior to the decline in numbers during 1987–88. Also, although breeding success showed a negative association with the year since 1988, the association was slight and far from significant.

On other areas also, most declines and extinctions occurred before 1988. This was before recent increases since 1990 in the number of breeding common gulls and non-breeding ravens as potential predators on plover eggs and chicks in some areas such as Corndavon, Morven Lodge and the Ladder Hills, and also lesser black-backed gulls (*Larus fuscus*) along the Lecht road across the Ladder Hills. Therefore, predation is not a general sufficient condition to start the declines, even though it is possible that it exacerbated some falls in numbers and led to earlier extinction than would otherwise have been the case.

Recent climatic warming in north-east Scotland is another possible cause of declines and extinctions. However, this warming has occurred since 1988. Most declines began before that. Hence, warming has not been sufficient to cause the declines or extinctions, although it remains possible that it has exacerbated some of them as above for predation.

Conclusion

There has been a general decline, in many areas to extinction. A likely cause is farm intensification on wintering grounds near the North Sea, especially permanent pasture converted to autumn-sown crops. This seems a sufficient condition for declines, though not necessary if one considers habitat loss or deterioration.

Acknowledgements

I thank gamekeepers Derek Calder, Bill Duncan, Willie Potts, Matt Ramage, John Robertson, David Scrimgeour, Fred Taylor, Alistair Thomson and Charles Wright, ranger Neil Cook, farmer Henry Auchnie, David Jenkins, Robert Moss and my father Adam Watson senior for useful observations.

References

Cook, M. (1992). The birds of Moray and Nairn. Mercat, Edinburgh.

Dennis, R. (1995). The birds of Badenoch and Strathspey. Colin Baxter, Photography, Grantown-on-Spey.

Gibbons, D.W., Amar, A., Anderson, G.Q.A., Bolton, M., Bradbury, R.B., Eaton, M.A., Evans, A.D., Grant, M.C., Gregory, R.D., Hilton, G.M., Hirons, G.J.M., Johnstone, I., Newbery, P., Peach, W.J., Ratcliffe, N., Smith, K.W., Summers, R.W., Walton, P. & Wilson, J.D. (2007). The predation of wild birds in the UK: a review of its conservation impact and management. Research report No 23, Royal Society for the Protection of Birds, Sandy.

Harding, N.J., Green, R.E. & Summers, R.W. (1994). The effects of future changes in land use on upland birds in Britain. Royal Society for the Protection of Birds, Sandy.

Jenkins, D., Watson, A. & Miller, G.R. (1967). Population fluctuations in the red grouse *Lagopus lagopus scoticus*. Journal of Animal Ecology 36, 97–122.

Jenkins, D. & Watson, A. (2001). Bird numbers in relation to grazing on a grouse moor from 1957–61 to 1988–98. Bird Study 48, 18–22.

Mountains to Marine Bird Survey Team (1999). Mar Lodge Estate breeding bird survey 30 May–13 June 1998. Report to National Trust for Scotland.

Nethersole-Thompson, D. (1952). A survey of the birds of Rothiemurchus Forest and western Cairngorms. Report to Royal Society for the Protection of Birds and the Nature Conservancy.

Nethersole-Thompson, D. & Watson, A. (1974). The Cairngorms. Collins, London.

Parr, R. (1990a). Population study of golden plover *Pluvialis apricaria* using marked birds. Ornis Scandinavica 11, 179–189.

Parr, R.A. (1990b). Moorland birds and their predators in relation to afforestation. Nature Conservancy Council Chief Scientist Directorate commissioned research report No 1081, Institute of Terrestrial Ecology, Banchory.

Parr, R.A. (1992a). Moorland birds and their predators in relation to afforestation. PhD thesis, University of Aberdeen.

Parr, R. (1992b). The decline to extinction of a population of golden plover in north-east Scotland. Ornis Scandinavica 23, 152–158.

Parr, R. (1993). Nest predation and numbers of golden plovers *Pluvialis apricaria* and other moorland waders. Bird Study 40, 223–231.

Rae, R. & Watson, A. (1998). Minimal numbers and habitat of breeding dunlin in north-east Scotland. Scottish Birds 19, 185–194.

Rae, R., Weston, E. & Duthie, E. (2011). Numbers and breeding success of golden plover and dunlin in an area frequented by ravens. Scottish Birds 31, 98–106.

Watson, A. (1965). A population study of ptarmigan (*Lagopus mutus*) in Scotland. Journal of Animal Ecology 34, 135–172.

Watson, A., Moss, R. & Rae, S. (1998). Population dynamics of Scottish rock ptarmigan cycles. Ecology 79, 1174–1192.

Watson, A. & O'Hare, P.J. (1979). Spacing behaviour of red grouse at low density on Irish bog. Ornis Scandinavica 10, 252–261.

Whitfield, D.P. (2002). Status of breeding dotterel (*Charadrius morinellus*) in Britain in 1999. Bird Study 49, 237–249.

Legend to Figure 1. Number of golden plover in May on 107-ha study area, Glas Maol, 1946–2012.

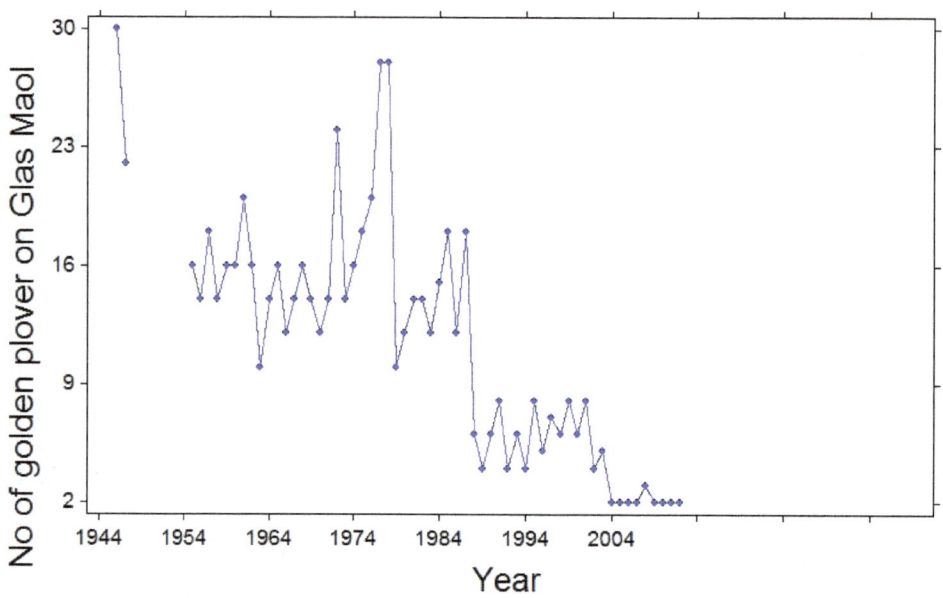

Table 1. Spring numbers of golden plover in relation to calendar year, negative sign shows decline. No area had tree-planting. Blank cells have same years and P as in first cell with such data above them.

Place	Span of years*	n of years	r_s	P
Derry Cairngorm	1944–99	56	−0.620	<0.0001
Morven Lodge	1944–12	46	−0.730	
Buailteach flocks		52	−0.898	
Glen Derry	1944–12	69	−0.831	
Glen Lui	1944–12		−0.801	
Braichlie–Pollagach	1944–12	15	−0.591	0.0232
Beinn Bhreac	1945–12	14	−0.836	0.0003
Cairn Lochan	1945–08	64	−0.507	<0.0001
Cac Carn Mor	1945–12	37	−0.829	
Abergeldie, Bad a' Chabair	1945–11	21	−0.769	0.0001
Abergeldie, Bovaglie	1945–12	13	−0.754	0.0044
Cairn Gorm, Allt Mor	1946–09	43	−0.786	<0.0001
Moine Bhealaidh	1946–12	22	−0.517	0.0147
Glas-choille		24	−0.642	0.0009
Glas Maol	1946–12	60	−0.818	<0.0001
Mar Lodge, Creag Bhalg	1948–12	12	−0.828	0.0014
Sron a' Cha-no	1949–09	34	−0.860	<0.0001
Kerloch V	1954–12	54	−0.397	0.0032
Glen Gairn, The Strone		47	−0.825	<0.0001
Corndavon, Coulachan		46	−0.772	
Spittal of Glenmuick		18	−0.709	0.0014
Glen Esk low I	1956–12	30	−0.643	0.0002
Glen Esk low IIA			−0.645	
Glen Esk low IIB			−0.648	
Glen Esk low III			−0.641	
Glen Esk low IV			−0.642	

Glen Esk low VIB			−0.644	
Glen Esk low V+VIA		40	−0.810	<0.0001
Crathie, Monaltrie Moss	1957–07	8	−0.903	0.0007
Dinnet, Roar Hill west	1957–12	12	−0.926	<0.0001
Dinnet, Morven south		7	−0.926	0.0118
Corndavon, Crathie Burn	1957–12	8	−0.825	0.0188
Glen Isla, Craighead	1958–09	11	−0.781	0.0070
Cairn Gorm, Allt na Ciste		10	−0.846	0.0035
Glen Esk, Cairn Robie	1958–12	29	−0.594	0.0008
Gannochy, Punchbowl		30	−0.736	<0.0001
Dinnet, Roar Hill	1959–12	8	−0.764	0.0391
Glen Dye, Aven	1960–91	8	−0.894	0.01
Glen Esk low VII	1960–12	28	−0.535	0.0038
Fettercairn, Whitelaws	1961–12	30	−0.767	<0.0001
Carn Aosda		52	−0.676	
Kerloch I		50	−0.842	
Kerloch II–IV and XI		46	−0.813	
Meall Odhar west	1963–12	50	−0.496	
Meall Odhar east			−0.882	
Meall Odhar Beag			−0.823	
Kerloch X	1964–12	28	−0.857	
Rickarton, Allochie		37	−0.392	0.0171
Rickarton, White Hill			−0.392	
Corgarff fields		49	−0.955	<0.0001
Kerloch XIII	1965–12	38	−0.806	
Beinn a' Bhuird	1968–12	28	−0.518	0.0060
Meikle Corr Riabhach	1969–12	15	−0.616	0.0163
Carn nan Sac		14	−0.913	<0.0001
Kerloch XIV	1970–12	38	−0.799	
Kerloch XV	1975–12	32	−0.678	
Corgarff, Delavine	1985–12	18	−0.789	0.0001

Gannochy, Fingray	1987–98	12	−0.762	0.0059
Gannochy, Colmeallie	1987–12	26	−0.588	0.0019
Gannochy, Corathro			−0.555	0.0038
Gannochy, Saddle			−0.462	0.0183
Gannochy, Leuchary	1987–11	25	−0.564	0.0038
Gannochy, Waggles	1987–12	26	−0.462	0.0183

* No data for some years in some spans.

Numbers in flocks in April–May on fields at Buailteach and Corgarff were annual daytime means, excluding dawns, dusks, and days with deep snow on nesting grounds. In 1946–2012, numbers in flocks during August fell at Glas Maol, Meall Odhar and Cairn Lochan ($n = 50$, 50 and 46, $r_s = -0.732$, -0.887 and -0.523, $P < 0.0001$, <0.0001 and 0.0002, last year of data 2012, 2012, 2009), at Ben Avon ($n = 10$, $r_s = -0.865$, $P = 0.0027$), at Beinn a' Bhuird in 1948–09, and at Carn an Tuirc in 1964–07 ($n = 8$, $r_s = -0.762$, $P = 0.0391$). Numbers seen in flocks during 1983–2012 by me and later D. Scrimgeour on grass fields at Corgarff Castle fell with the year ($n = 14$, $r_s = -0.641$, $P = 0.0154$)

Rae et al. (2011) surveyed golden plover at Cairn of Claise in 2010. Robert Rae and I found two pairs with young in 1987 at places where Rae et al. recorded none in 2010.

Chapter 6. Evidence of no material increase of breeding dotterel in 1940s–90s

Until 1987–88, authors' estimates of dotterel (*Charadrius morinellus*) numbers in Scotland rested on extrapolation from their fieldwork on a small proportion of the potential habitat. This applied to the earliest estimate that 80–100 pairs might breed in Scotland (Blackwood 1920). It applied to an estimate of 60–80 pairs in Britain (Nethersole-Thompson & Nethersole-Thompson 1961), although they also used notes given to them by other observers. Extrapolation from fieldwork up to 1986 on a much bigger proportion of the potential habitat led to a rough estimate of at least 600 pairs in Scotland, and 'it is suggested that the main reason for this higher figure is better survey technique' (Watson & Rae 1987, for brevity called WR below). WR thought that there might be 1000 pairs, but they were conservative, especially about the Cairngorms and the Mounth, because these two massifs had the largest area of potential habitat and much of it had not been searched well. Then came the first national Scottish survey by many observers in 1987–88, showing more than 840 pairs (Galbraith *et al.* 1993).

When WR gave two examples of no change between the late 1940s and the 1980s, they judged that giving more would be superfluous, because their experience generally indicated no material change. Evidence on a third case of no change was mentioned incidentally in a paper on a population study (Watson 1988), and likewise three more cases showing little change from the mid 1960s to the late 1980s (Watson 1989).

Table 1 collates these six cases, and others hitherto unpublished. The evidence shows that numbers in the 1940s–70s did not differ materially from those in the late 1980s. No material change is the most parsimonious hypothesis, and the sole one with data from the same observers, areas, and methods in both the early and later periods. In studies of plants and animals, the norm is that more effort reveals more individuals seen and a wider distribution than was formerly known. An example is that more American birds are now seen in Britain. As Bill Bourne wisely stated (1979), 'It seems possible as with American migrants some of these birds have always occurred but were not accepted in the past, though they are now picked up and confirmed because of their increased accessibility, better fieldwork, and an improved reporting system'. Hence to claim an increase in such cases, as in dotterel, is unrealistic, given the obviously greater effort than previously.

Likewise, to claim a decline is unrealistic and invalid if observer effort has fallen or if methods and observers have changed. Yet a decline of dotterel in Scotland since the 1991 paper has been claimed from a survey in 1999 (Whitfield 2002; Shaw *et al.* 2006), despite an obvious large reduction of effort, as well as large changes in methods and observers for the 1999 survey.

During summer 2011, the RSPB and SNH are doing a fresh survey, now the third dotterel survey in Scotland by SNH. They issued a press release, taken up e.g. by Paterson (2011) and Ross (2011), in which an ornithologist officer of SNH is

Cock dotterel on eggs, The Mounth south of Braemar, June 1987 said to be 'encouraging walkers to report any sightings of the mountain birds to help with the survey'. Because the first two SNH surveys did not involve sightings reported by walkers, this call to walkers for the third survey is a large change in methods and observer effort. Thereby it invalidates the third survey as a reliable basis for comparison with the two earlier SNH surveys.

More formally for the present paper, the null hypothesis is that there has been no long-term rise or fall in numbers, and hence no difference. The alternative or working hypothesis is that there has been a large increase. The evidence goes against the alternative and confirms the null. Evidence against, or refutation, is more reliable than evidence for, or confirmation (Popper 1959).

In short, there is no good evidence of a big increase, or of a big subsequent decline. No evidence of material change is the realistic and parsimonious conclusion.

Appendix

Five estimates by authors whose evidence did not come from their own fieldwork.

1. D. Nethersole-Thompson (1973), probably >100 pairs 'in recent years of exceptionally high numbers', after AW informed DNT about many birds seen by AW in his population studies on defined areas since 1965. For instance, WR stated 'Indeed, A.W. saw numbers greater than one of the previous estimated totals for Britain (60–80 pairs) in one spring on only five hills, including the three study-area hills'. This was in May 1971, just before egg-laying.

2. D. Nethersole-Thompson (1983), 100–150 pairs 'in good years in 1970s'. This statement repeated 1 above.

3. D. & M. Nethersole-Thompson (1986), 'from 1970 onwards numbers have possibly increased to 100–150 pairs in favourable years'. This again repeated 1.

4. Thom (1986), in her general review of all bird species in Scotland, 'estimates the current Scottish total as 100–150 pairs, so there has clearly been some recent increase'. Note DNT's caution with 'probably' in 1, 'good years' in 2, and 'possibly.... in favourable years' in 3, whereas Thom omitted his caution, added 'clearly', and hence overstated.

5. D. Ratcliffe (1990) reported 500+ pairs increasing, but gave no data from his or others' fieldwork. The 500+ value was incorrect, in view of, a) WR, b) the 1987–88 survey (Galbraith *et al.*), and c) the newsletters about the survey, sent annually from 1987 to observers and to Ratcliffe. Ratcliffe adduced no data to back his use of the term 'increasing'. Likewise,

Juvenile dotterel beside wires of derelict sheep fence, The Mounth, August 1972

he presented an estimate of 10000 pairs of ptarmigan for Britain, despite failing to back it with evidence of personal fieldwork by him or others. I have found no data in the literature giving a ptarmigan count by him on a defined area, and no transect count of ptarmigan by him. Surprisingly, his opinion was accepted uncritically in a recent review giving population estimates for all bird species in Britain (Baker *et al.* 2006).

Review of publications in 1990–2006

Whitfield *et al.* (1991) noted WR's emphasis on periods when dotterel are more readily visible. Referring to the high estimate in the 1987–88 survey reported later by Galbraith *et al.*, they stated, 'Again, the primary reason for the large difference between the....estimate and Nethersole-Thompson's estimates was believed to be the superior recent surveys'. However, they then wrote, 'the few sites covered with comparable effort since the 1930s 'now have more birds. Yet their phrases 'comparable effort' and 'superior recent surveys' were contradictory. They stated that late snow in Norway may have shifted more birds to nest in Scotland, but gave no evidence on snow or on shifting.

Galbraith *et al.* attributed their high estimate partly to a 'genuine' increase, suggesting 'the population has increased, but by a percentage that cannot be determined'. If a percentage cannot be determined, the claim of an increase is invalid, as is the claim that the population has increased.

They stated incorrectly that birds were more abundant and widespread 'than hitherto estimated'. On abundance, this ignored WR's statements of 'at least' 600 pairs and WR's + for numbers in each area

AW senior on dotterel ground in east Cairngorms, August 1975

(e.g. 30+). On distribution, it ignored WR's distribution area being no less widespread than in the national 1987–88 survey.

Galbraith *et al.* claimed that dotterel were more abundant in the east Highlands than estimated 'even by Watson & Rae'. This was incorrect, because it again ignored WR's statements on abundance as explained in the above paragraph,

Moreover, Galbraith *et al.* wrote that 'population size has virtually doubled on some tops', risen from nil on some 'where there were no breeding Dotterel in the 1960s', and stayed the same on others. All three claims conflicted with their statements about 'superior recent surveys' and the recent 'greater effort'. Also, it was invalid to claim 'there were no breeding' birds, rather than 'no birds were recorded'.

Galbraith *et al.* (1993) repeated the assertion that snow in Norway caused more passing birds to nest in Scotland, again without giving evidence on snow. They mentioned unpublished data indicating 'a marked increase in numbers of birds passing through Britain since the late 1950s', but this could be said of American birds and many other cases where apparent increases are confounded with greater observer effort.

Also they wrote, 'the techniques used by some observers re-visiting tops over several decades have not changed in a way that explains no change in some areas but increases in others'. This assumed unrealistically that skills do not change with an observer's practice and with competition among observers searching together, and that efficiency does not vary with time of season, time of day, weather, area size, observer numbers, observers' experience of dotterel, and above all the observers' vigilance and concentration.

Galbraith *et al* wrote that early published estimates before 1987, the year of WR's paper, were not 'put forward as being comprehensive', and 'conclusions reached by ornithologists that these estimates are low are hardly surprising!'. However, the phrases just quoted by me in this paragraph contradicted their claims of an increase since these earlier estimates.

They stated that some 'tops have been visited frequently since the mid-1950s', but four of the six references that they gave were reviews that stressed the nesting season and gave no long-term counts from the authors' own fieldwork, a fifth was about the nesting season in mid June 1976–80 (P.S. Thompson 1983, *Scottish Birds* 190), and the sixth was WR who stated that birds skulk and are easily overlooked during the nesting period. The main aim of most authors in publications before 1987 was to find nests, not to count numbers on defined areas and assess breeding success there.

Galbraith *et al.* claimed that some of these tops previously 'were covered by experienced observers'. This ignored the data in WR showing that experienced observers can easily overlook nesting birds, especially in warm midday sunshine. It omitted that I saw more birds after 1965 when I started studying numbers and breeding success on defined areas.

Thompson & Whitfield (1993) repeated, again without evidence, the claim that late snow in Norway caused more dotterel to stop in Scotland. They wrote that Britain's climate cooled in the 1960s and 70s, without giving climatic data or sources. They omitted any reference to climate in the 1980s, the decade that included the Galbraith *et al.* survey of 1987–88.

Also they stated, 'Breeding densities have at least doubled on some hills', but this was invalid because they gave no data from the same methods and the same observers in both periods. Their phrase 'at least doubled' also contradicts the phrase in Galbraith *et al.* that 'population size has virtually doubled on some tops'.

Thompson & Whitfield wrote of 'a higher tendency for Dotterels to settle and breed', without adducing evidence of such higher tendency. They noted that WR 'argue that now more birdwatchers detect more Dotterels', but WR gave this only as a secondary aspect of observer effort, which applied to sites that had not been visited in early years. It did not apply to the higher numbers seen by WR on areas where other observers had previously seen fewer dotterel. Galbraith *et al.*, and Thompson & Whitfield ignored most of WR's points on methods, and WR's and Watson's (1988, 1989) data showing no change on several areas.

Thompson *et al.* (1996) wrote that early assessments were probably underestimates, but 'it is possible that there has been an increase in some parts'. One could as well state 'no change' or 'a decrease', since no rigorous evidence demonstrating an increase had yet been published.

Whitfield (2002) stated that a national survey by SNH in 1999 revealed a big decline since SNH's first survey in the late 1980s. However, methods and observers in 1999 differed materially from those in 1987–88. Even on the few intensively studied areas (their Fig. 5), the same observers and effort as in 1987–88 were not used in most of the later years. This

Sheep on dotterel ground, The Mounth, September 1964 after dotterel left for Africa

Dotterel ground, north Cairngorms, 20 September 1998 after dotterel left for Africa

Field observations over decades 87

need not have happened if some of the experienced observers in the early survey had been asked to help with later surveys. Because of material changes in observers and methods, claims of a big decline from 1987–88 to 1999 are therefore unwarranted and not reliable.

Even the large total in 1987–88 was probably an underestimate for reasons to do with observer inexperience. In several cases known to me, volunteers who lacked experience of dotterel were allocated to certain hills, and reported no dotterel. Yet, during every year when I or Robert Rae (i.e. WR) visited these hills before and since, we found birds.

Shaw *et al.* (2006) stated 'Britain's Dotterel population….has evidently increased substantially since the 1950s…. However, part of this 'increase' may be due to a growing level of survey effort in the past 20 years'. Despite having made this qualification about greater observer effort, the authors then contradicted it by asserting, 'The reasons for the Dotterel's population increase up to the late 1980s…. are unclear'. Having stated that dotterel numbers nationally had shown a big decline by 1999 (referring to Whitfield 2002), they next gave data from six areas in the Cairngorms where more intensive work had been done annually. However, they then left matters unclear by stating that work on the six areas 'yielded mixed trends during 1986–99', and only one area, at East Drumochter, showed 'a marked decline, attributed mainly to localised' predation on eggs by ravens. In fact, numbers at the other five areas fluctuated without any obvious trend up or down. Hence the lack of any trend conflicted with the decline that they claimed from national surveys. This contradiction was left unexplained, increasing the dubiety of the claimed national decline.

References

Baker, H., Stroud, D.A., Aebischer, N.J., Cranswick, P.A., Gregory, R.D., McSorley, C.A., Noble, D.G. & Rehfisch, M.M. (2006). Population estimates of birds in Great Brtain and the United Kingdom. British Birds 99, 25–44.

Blackwood, C.G.. (1920). Notes on the breeding habits of the dotterel *Eudromias morinellus* in Scotland. Scottish Naturalist 98, 185–194.

Bourne, W.R.P. (1979). Colonization of Scotland by northern birds. Scottish Birds 10, 282–283.

Galbraith, H., Murray, S., Rae, S., Whitfield, D.P. & Thompson, D.B.A. (1993). Numbers and distribution of dotterel *Charadrius morinellus* breeding in Great Britain. Bird Study 40, 161–169.

Gordon, S. (1915). Hill birds of Scotland. Arnold, London.

Nethersole-Thompson, D. & C. (1961). Dotterel. In: The birds of the British Isles (by D.A. Bannerman), 10, pp. 246–253. Oliver & Boyd, Edinburgh & London.

Nethersole-Thompson, D. (1973). The dotterel. Collins, London.

Nethersole-Thompson, D. (1983). Birds of the western Palearctic (Ed. by S. Cramp & K.E.L. Simmons), p. 3, Oxford University Press.

Nethersole-Thompson, D. & M. (1986). Waders. Poyser, Calton.

Paterson, L. (2011). Mountain bird sightings wanted. Press & Journal, 15 July.

Popper, K.R. (1959). The logic of scientific discovery. Hutchinson, London.

Ratcliffe, D. (1990). Bird life of mountain and upland. Cambridge University Press.

Ross, J. (2011). Rare birds 'running out of places to go'. The Scotsman, 15 July.

Shaw, P., Thompson, D.B.A, Duncan, K. & Buxton, N. (2006). Birds. In: The nature of the Cairngorms (Ed. by P. Shaw & D.B.A. Thompson), pp. 293–339. Stationery Office, Edinburgh.

Thom, V.M. (1986). Birds in Scotland. Poyser, Calton.

Thompson, D.B.A., Watson, A., Rae, S. & Boobyer, G. (1996). Recent changes in breeding bird populations in the Cairngorms. Botanical Journal of Scotland 48, 99–110.

Thompson, D.B.A. & Whitfield, D.P. (1993). Dotterel. In: The new atlas of breeding birds in Britain and Ireland: 1988-91 (Ed. by D.W. Gibbons, J.B. Reid & R.A. Chapman), pp. 166–167. Poyser, London.

Watson, A. (1988). Dotterel *Charadrius morinellus* numbers in relation to human impact in Scotland. Biological Conservation 43, 245–256.

Watson, A. (1989). Dotterel populations and spacing on three Scottish areas in 1967–86. Ornis Fennica 66, 85–99.

Watson, A. & Rae, R. (1987). Dotterel numbers, habitat and breeding success in Scotland. Scottish Birds 14, 191–198.

Whitfield, D.P. (2002). The status of breeding dotterel *Charadrius morinellus* in Britain in 1999. Bird Study 49, 237–249.

Whitfield, D.P., Duncan, K., Murray, S., Rae, S., Smith, R. & Thompson, D.B.A. (1991). Monitoring the dotterel population of Great Britain. In: Britain's birds in 1989/90: the Conservation and Monitoring Review (Ed. by D. Stroud & D. Glue), 109–111. British Trust for Ornithology & Nature Conservancy Council, Peterborough.

Table 1. Number of pairs seen on parts of certain hills, a dash indicating no data.

	late 40s	50s	60s	70s	80s	90s
Derry Cairngorm"	4	4,5,5	4,5,5,5	5	5	-
Lochnagar east	-	-	4	5	4	-
Beinn Iutharn Mhor	3	-	-	3	-	-
Carn an Tuirc	-	-	3	2	3	-
Garbh Uisge Beag^	3	3	3–4	3–4	3–4	3
Carn Cloich-mhuilinn	-	3	-	-	3	-
Carn Liath, Inverey	-	2	-	-	3	3
Braid Cairn	-	2,2	2,3	-	2	-
Buidheanach of Cairntoul	2	-	3	2	2	-
Beinn Bhreac"	2	2	-	3	-	-
Moine Bhealaidh	-	2	-	2	-	-
The Devil's Point	2	-	1	-	2	-
Sgor Dubh, Luibeg	-	1	-	-	1	-
Lochan Buidhe	1,1	1,1	1	1	1	1
Allt Clach nan Taillear	1	1	-	1	1	1
Naked Hill	-	1,1	1,1	-	1	-
Coire Cas top#	-	1	1	0	0	0,1

" In Watson & Rae (1987).

^ In Watson (1988), 3–4 pairs annually in 1967–87, in most years 3.

None seen in 1970s–80s, attributed to walkers damaging the ground (Watson 1988).
If one compares the mean for each hill in the 1940s–60s with the later mean (excluding Coire Cas top, where trampling by walkers severely damaged the vegetation in the 1970s and later, the two do not differ significantly ($n = 16$, paired $t = -1.30$, $P = 0.21$).

Gordon (1915) noted a 'score or so' on Braeriach after a June snowfall in the 1910s, indicating numbers as high as in recent decades.

Chapter 7. Some counts of birds on moorland and alpine land

Most published counts of birds on moorland and alpine land have been done in the birds' breeding season. This is not an ideal timing, because individuals of many species skulk when incubating eggs or when they have chicks, and are then easily overlooked. In this Chapter below, all references to published studies involved fieldwork during the breeding season, except for papers by AW, David Jenkins and Robert Moss of the former grouse research team.

Our papers rested on fieldwork before the breeding season, when birds were still fairly conspicuous. Counts of red grouse and ptarmigan during the nesting season and the season of small chicks can be attempted using trained pointing dogs, and on small areas with intensive searching can be accurate, especially if many adults are individually recognisable in the field by coloured back-tabs or coloured rings. However, in general they are inaccurate and unreliable, The counts usually underestimate the total values known from just before the breeding season, and again from late in the breeding season when the birds have large or fully grown chicks and all birds can be found accurately using dogs.

We generally did our counts on low moorland during late March and the start of April, on high moorland from the end of March to the middle of April, and on alpine land in April and the start of May. The timing varied according to the weather of any one year, early in a warm spring, later in a snowy frosty spring.

Several broad surveys have been done to assess bird numbers in the breeding season on moorland, for instance in north-east Scotland (e.g. Brown & Shepherd 1993; Brown & Stillman 1993). The method of Brown & Shepherd is frequently cited. However, the authors continually used the terms 'census' and 'censuses', when this was wholly invalid. All that they obtained were counts, and the proportions that these counts formed of the total numbers present remained unknown. They stated that 'Censuses were conducted between 08.30 and 18.00 hours, thus avoiding the main periods of rapidly changing bird activity'. Hence the observers concentrated on the main hours of high daytime, when waders and other species are least likely to be conspicuous visually and by voice. Also, there was a bias towards late afternoon, when air temperatures are often at their highest for the day and birds are correspondingly less active and more inclined to skulk unseen and unheard.

This was perverse and counter-productive, because Reed *et al.* (1983) had long demonstrated these issues and quantified them for dunlin in the breeding season and later Reed *et al.* (1985) at four moorland study areas in County Durham and Sutherland for dunlin, golden plover, curlew, lapwing, and snipe, again in the breeding season. Reed *et al.* (1985) concluded 'In Co. Durham all four species had significantly more records in the early morning (<0900h) than in normal hours (0900–1700 h) or the evening (>1700 h). Large-scale comparative surveys will be biased if their data include transects started early in the morning as well as later in the day. The most efficient surveys will be those carried out on a limited area in the first few hours after dawn'. Also they cited Skirvin (1981), who pointed out that for birds more generally the detectability of bird species is highest in the early part of the day, dropping to a low point in the early afternoon before rising to a second, though lower, peak in the early evening.

To this I would add that the most accurate results of surveys without dogs come from using numbers and locations of birds heard calling in semi-darkness at the dawn or dusk chorus. This is before sunrise and after sunset (see Watson & O' Hare 1979b), further discussed below.

The Brown & Shepherd method is not the only dubious unacceptable study in the field of wader numbers in the breeding season. Woolly thinking and uncritical assumptions marred a paper by Haworth & Thompson (1990). They reported fewer wader species and lower abundance near paths and tracks in the Peak District than away from paths and tracks. This led them to state the uncritical assertion that this was evidence showing the adverse effects of human disturbance, mainly from walkers, on the occurrence and abundance of wading birds. The obvious point did not occur to them, although any gamekeeper or tracks engineer could have told them, that paths and tracks do not occur at random, but avoid wet ground, especially thick wet peat. Of course the wader species favour exactly these wet conditions, and are bound therefore to avoid paths and tracks even when no walkers are on them. Unfortunately, the National Park Board accepted these invalid assertions and other uncritical evidence from studies of golden plover, and decided to propose banning walkers from certain areas during the breeding season of the waders. A report by Watson (1991), commissioned by the Ramblers' Association, presented a critique of all the above uncritical invalid evidence. When the Board received it, they abandoned the proposal to ban walkers.

Few intensive studies have been reported where the authors obtained total counts of all birds present on moorland. One example of an intensive study was research by Jenkins & Watson (2001) on low moorland near Tarfside in Glen Esk, Angus. Their main work there was on red grouse, and they obtained total counts or total enumerations by using pointing dogs and other methods. Jenkins & Watson also used the pointing dogs to find other birds during the counts of red grouse. Watson later used dog counts to assess the abundance of red grouse on wet moorland at Glenamoy, Co Mayo (Watson & O' Hare 1979a). The results from the dog counts were compared with the numbers of singing birds as heard and located by a team of observers at the dawn and dusk chorus (Watson & O' Hare 1979b). This showed close agreement between the two methods, when allowance was made for doubling the number of singing birds. Effectively the number of singers fitted the number of pairs, for skylark, snipe, golden plover, mallard, teal, and indeed every species encountered.

In this Chapter I present some counts of birds on moorland and alpine land, mostly in north-east Scotland. Many observations came from moorland close to but higher than the low moorland or 'Low' study area of Jenkins *et al.* (1963). This was their 'High' study area and yet higher areas 'Intermediate' (on Hill of Gairney), and 'Boundary' (on Braid Cairn, which rose into alpine land on its uppermost part). Jenkins *et al.* (1963) divided the 1000-acre High area into four parts A, B, C and D. B covered the catchment of the upper Easter Burn including Hill of Saughs, A was further east and lower down the Easter Burn, C on Hill of Kirny, and D from Badalair across to Corrie Duff.

Other study areas for red grouse lay at Punchbowl at Gannochy Estate in lower Glen Esk, in Glen Isla, at Glen Tarken by Loch Earn, at Dirnanean near Enochdhu in Strath Ardle, at Sands of Forvie by the North Sea, and in upper Deeside. I present here some counts of birds other than red grouse (the data on red grouse have long been published elsewhere in the papers noted below in this paragraph) at Glen Muick (below Craig Vallich), by the Coulachan Burn on the Corndavon beat of Invercauld, and in upper Glen Girnock (erroneously called 'Lochnagar' by Jenkins et al. (1963). Jenkins et al. (1963) described these areas and those in the previous paragraph in some detail (including altitudes, locations and bedrock) and mapped them. Subsequently, Miller et al. (1966) gave further details on vegetation. Since then we used other study areas for red grouse at Kerloch moor by Strachan near Banchory (Jenkins et al. 1967; Watson, Moss, Rothery & Parr 1984), as well as some of those mentioned above, including sub-alpine moorland at the Cairnwell (Moss et al. 1975), during experiments involving applications of fertiliser (Watson et al. 1977; Watson, Moss & Parr 1984), and during an experiment with a change in land management on Mull (Watson et al. 1987). Our next main study area after Kerloch for research on red grouse was at Rickarton moor near Stonehaven, close to the North Sea coast (Watson et al. 1988; Moss et al. 1996).

Below, I present also counts of birds other than ptarmigan (as for red grouse, the data on ptarmigan have already been published elsewhere in the papers listed in the next sentence) on several alpine study areas for ptarmigan. The areas have been described, including altitudes, locations and bedrock as above, and also were mapped (Watson 1965, 1979; Watson et al. 1998). One can obtain total counts of all ptarmigan when the birds are dispersed and strongly territorial in April, even when the ground is frozen or covered in light snow. This is also the case for red grouse in April, though such wintry conditions occur less frequently on high or sub-alpine moorland than on alpine land. In such conditions, other species such as meadow pipits are often temporarily absent, returning quickly as the snow vanishes and the ground thaws out. I have excluded from the Tables any counts in such conditions.

References

Brown, A.F. & Shepherd, K.B. (1993). A method for censusing upland breeding waders. Bird Study 40, 189–195.

Brown, A.F. & Stillman, RA. (1993). Bird-habitat associations in the eastern Highlands of Scotland. Journal of Applied Ecology 30, 31–42.

Haworth, P.F. & Thompson, D.B.A. (1990). Factors associated with the breeding distribution of upland birds in the south Pennines, England. Journal of Applied Ecology 27, 562–577.

Jenkins, D., Watson, A. & Miller, G.R. (1963). Population studies on red grouse, Lagopus lagopus scoticus (Lath.) in north-east Scotland. Journal of Animal Ecology 32, 317–376.

Jenkins, D., Watson, A. & Miller, G.R. (1967). Population fluctuations in the red grouse Lagopus lagopus scoticus. Journal of Animal Ecology 36, 97–122.

Jenkins, D. & Watson, A. (2001). Bird numbers in relation to grazing on a grouse moor from 1957–161 to 1988–1998. Bird Study 48, 18–122.

Miller, G.R., Jenkins, D. & Watson, A.(1966). Heather performance and red grouse populations. I Visual estimates of heather performance. Journal of Applied Ecology 3, 313–326.

Moss, R., Watson, A. & Parr, R. (1996). Experimental prevention of a population cycle in red grouse. Ecology 77, 1512–1530.

Reed, T.M., Barrett, C., Barrett, J., Hayhow, S. & Minshull, B. (1985). Diurnal variability in the detection of waders on their breeding grounds. Bird Study 32, 71–74.

Reed, T.M., Barrett, J.C., Barrett, C. & Langslow, D.R. (1983). Diurnal variability in the detection of dunlin *Calidris alpina*. Bird Study 30, 244–246.

Skirvin, A.A. (1981). Effect of the time of day and time of season on the numbers of observations and density estimates of breeding birds. In: Estimating numbers of terrestrial birds. Studies in Avian Biology 6 (Ed. by C.J. Ralph & J.M. Scott), 271–274, Lawrence, Kansas.

Watson, A. (1965). A population study of ptarmigan (*Lagopus mutus*) in Scotland. Journal of Animal Ecology 34, 135–172.

Watson, A. (1979). Bird and mammal numbers in relation to human impact at ski lifts on Scottish hills. Journal of Applied Ecology 16, 753–764.

Watson, A (1991). Critique of Report 'Moorland recreation and wildlife in the Peak District' by Penny Anderson, Peak Park Joint Planning Board 1990. 25pp. The Ramblers' Association, London.

Watson, A., Moss, R. & Parr, R. (1987). Grouse increase on Mull. Landowning in Scotland 207, 6.

Watson, A., Moss, R. & Parr, R. (1984). Effects of food enrichment on numbers and spacing behaviour of red grouse. Journal of Animal Ecology 53, 663–678.

Watson, A., Moss, R., Parr, R., Trenholm, I.B. & Robertson, A. (1988). Preventing a population decline in red grouse (*Lagopus lagopus scoticus*) by manipulating density. Experientia 44, 274–275.

Watson, A., Moss, R., Phillips, J. & Parr, R. (1977). The effect of fertilizers on red grouse stocks on Scottish moors grazed by sheep, cattle and deer. In: Écologie du Petit Gibier (Ed. by P. Pesson & M.G. Birkan), pp. 193–212. Gauthier-Villars, Paris.

Watson, A., Moss, R., Rothery, P. & Parr, R. (1984). Demographic causes and predictive models of population fluctuations in red grouse. Journal of Animal Ecology 53, 639–662.

Watson, A., Moss, R. & Rae, S. (1998). Population dynamics of Scottish rock ptarmigan cycles. Ecology 79, 1174–1192.

Watson, A. & O' Hare, P.J. (1979a). Red grouse populations on experimentally treated and untreated Irish bog. Journal of Applied Ecology 16, 433–452.

Watson, A. & O'Hare, P.J. (1979b). Spacing behaviour of red grouse at low density on Irish bog. Ornis Scandinavica 10, 252–261.

Appendix. Counts of birds on moorland and alpine land, no of pairs unless stated otherwise

Table 1. Glen Esk 'High' area of Jenkins *et al.* (1963), 121 ha each except D 42 ha.

Glen Esk High	A					B				C				D			
Year	57	58	59	60	61	58	59	60	61	58	59	60	61	58	59	60	61
Meadow pipit	8	10	8	8	17	8	9	8	13	13	15	10	14	9	10	9	13
Golden plover	5	4	7	3	4	5	9	4	4	3	4	3	3	1	1	1	1
Curlew	5	4	3	2	2	2	1	1	1	2	2	2	2	1	1	1	1
Lapwing	5	3	3	2	2	1	2	1	1	1	4	3	1	1	1	1	1
Snipe	2	1	2	3	2	2	3	2	3	1	2	1	2	1	1	2	1
Dunlin	0	1	1	1	1	1	1	1	1	0	0	0	0	0	0	0	0
Wheatear	0	2	2	4	3	1	1	1	1	2	2	2	3	1	2	1	1
Skylark	0	1	2	4	1	1	1	1	1	2	1	2	1	1	1	1	1
Short-eared owl	0	1	0	0	1	0	0	0	0	0	0	0	0	0	0	0	0
Redshank	0	0	0	0	0	0	0	0	1	0	0	0	0	0	0	0	0
Mallard	0	0	0	0	3	0	0	0	0	0	0	0	0	0	0	0	0
Teal	0	0	0	0	0	0	0	0	0	1	0	0	0	0	0	0	0
Total	25	26	27	26	35	20	26	18	24	25	30	23	26	15	17	16	19

Table 2. Red grouse areas, 1 Punchbowl, 2 Braid Cairn, 3 Gairney, 4 Glen Isla, 1 & 4 121 ha each, 2 194 ha, 3 105 ha.

	1				2				3			4			
Year	58	59	60	61	58	59	60	61	59	60	61	58	59	60	61
Meadow pipit	10	13	35	5	9	10	9	13	4	7	8	3	6	14	7
Golden plover	3	6	6	7	1	2	2	2	2	1	2	1	2	1	3
Curlew	2	2	2	1	2	1	1	1	0	0	0	2	2	1	2
Lapwing	2	1	3	4	1	2	1	1	1	1	2	1	1	0	2
Snipe	2	3	4	4	0	0	0	0	0	0	0	0	1	2	1
Wheatear	1	1	1	1	2	1	2	1	1	1	1	0	1	1	1
Skylark	4	5	6	4	0	0	0	0	0	0	0	3	6	15	6
Short-eared owl	0	0	0	0	0	0	0	0	0	0	0	2	0	0	1
Redshank	0	0	0	0	0	0	0	0	1	2	2	0	0	0	0
Ptarmigan	0	0	0	0	0	2	0	0	0	0	0	0	0	0	0
Ring ouzel	1	1	2	2	0	0	0	0	0	0	0	0	0	0	0
Black grouse (birds)	0	0	0	0	0	0	0	0	0	0	0	15	17	1	0
Grey partridge	0	0	0	0	0	0	0	0	0	0	0	0	0	1	0
Dotterel	0	0	0	0	2	2	2	3	1	1	1	0	0	0	0
Dunlin	0	0	0	0	0	0	0	0	1	1	1	0	0	0	0
Mallard	0	0	0	0	0	0	0	0	0	0	3	0	0	0	2
Teal	0	0	0	0	0	0	0	0	0	0	3	0	0	0	0
Total	25	32	59	28	15	18	15	19	9	12	15	19	27	35	24

Table 3. Red grouse area Sands of Forvie 73 ha.

Year	58	59	60	61	62	63	64	65	66	67	68	69	70	71
Meadow pipit	4	4	4	5	4	4	9	6	4	7	8	5	6	10
Golden plover	0	3	0	0	0	0	0	0	0	0	0	0	0	0
Oystercatcher	0	0	1	0	0	0	0	0	0	0	0	0	0	0
Lapwing	0	2	0	0	0	0	0	0	0	0	0	0	0	0
Curlew	0	0	0	1	0	0	0	0	0	0	0	0	0	0
Snipe	0	0	0	1	0	0	0	0	0	0	0	0	0	0
Skylark	10	6	6	7	6	5	7	5	6	6	6	5	6	9
Short-eared owl	0	1	0	0	0	0	0	0	0	0	0	0	0	0
Total	14	16	11	14	10	9	16	11	10	13	14	10	12	19

Golden plover did not stay in 1956.

Table 4. Red grouse area Corndavon, Coulachan Burn 93 ha.

Year	57	58	59	60	61	62	63	64	65	66	67	68	69	70	71
Meadow pipit	8	14	17	15	15	13	5	11	15	17	20	19	20	10	6
Golden plover	5	4	6	5	8	5	4	4	4	8	8	4	8	6	12
Curlew	2	1	1	1	1	1	1	1	1	1	1	1	1	1	1
Lapwing	2	1	1	1	1	1	1	1	1	1	1	1	1	1	1
Snipe	3	1	1	1	2	1	1	1	1	2	1	2	2	2	2
Wheatear	1	1	1	1	1	1	1	2	1	1	1	1	1	1	2
Skylark	9	4	4	4	2	7	3	4	3	3	2	2	2	2	1
Wren	1	0	0	0	0	0	0	0	0	0	0	0	0	0	0
Short-eared owl	0	0	0	0	0	0	0	0	0	0	0	0	0	0	1
Redshank	0	0	0	0	0	0	0	0	0	0	0	0	0	1	1
Mallard	0	0	0	0	0	0	0	0	0	0	0	0	0	0	0
Teal	0	0	0	0	0	0	0	0	0	0	0	1	0	0	0
Ring ouzel	1	1	1	1	1	1	1	1	1	1	1	1	1	1	1
Grey partridge	0	1	0	0	0	0	0	0	0	0	0	0	0	0	0
Dunlin	1	0	1	1	1	1	0	1	1	1	1	1	1	0	1
Total	33	28	33	30	32	31	17	26	28	35	36	32	38	25	29

Table 5. Red grouse area Glen Girnock, erroneously 'Lochnagar' of Jenkins *et al.* (1963), 101 ha.

Year	61	62	63	64	65	66	67	68	69	70	71
Meadow pipit	20	17	8	18	9	10	12	9	12	8	12
Golden plover	5	3	2	2	2	6	4	3	2	4	7
Curlew	1	1	1	1	1	1	1	1	1	1	1
Lapwing	2	1	1	2	1	1	2	0	2	0	1
Snipe	3	6	1	2	1	3	2	2	2	3	4
Wheatear	1	1	1	1	1	1	1	1	1	1	1
Skylark	11	8	11	13	9	7	7	6	2	2	4
Short-eared owl	1	0	0	0	0	0	0	0	0	0	0
Redshank	1	0	0	0	0	0	0	0	0	0	0
Woodcock	0	0	0	0	0	0	0	0	0	0	1
Mallard	0	0	1	0	0	0	0	0	0	0	0
Teal	0	0	0	0	0	0	0	0	2	0	0
Total	45	37	26	39	24	29	29	22	24	19	32

Table 6. Red grouse area Glen Muick, Craig Vallich 121 ha.

Year	58	59	60	61	62	63	64	65	66	67	68	69	70	71
Meadow pipit	11	17	24	22	18	15	21	20	19	18	18	12	18	20
Golden plover	2	2	1	3	2	1	2	2	3	2	2	2	2	4
Curlew	1	1	1	2	1	1	2	1	1	1	1	1	1	2
Lapwing	1	1	3	1	1	1	2	2	1	1	1	1	1	2
Snipe	2	4	3	2	2	2	4	2	3	2	3	2	1	2
Wheatear	1	1	1	1	1	1	1	1	1	1	1	1	1	1
Skylark	3	2	3	4	3	3	5	5	4	4	4	4	3	5
Ring ouzel	1	0	0	0	0	0	1	0	0	0	0	0	0	1
Short-eared owl	1	0	0	1	0	0	0	1	0	1	0	0	0	0
Total	23	28	36	36	28	24	38	34	32	30	30	23	27	37

One black grouse in 1961

Table 7. Red grouse areas A Glen Tarken, B Dirnanean, C Corndavon II Creag Mhor, D Glenshee Lodge, 121, 84, 100, 100 ha.

	A			B		C		D
Year	59	60	61	60	61	58	59	60
Meadow pipit	36	13	11	3	3	11	12	11
Golden plover	0	0	0	1	2	4	5	2
Curlew	2	1	1	2	2	0	0	2
Lapwing	0	0	0	1	1	1	4	1
Snipe	2	1	1	1	1	0	0	0
Wheatear	2	3	1	1	1	1	1	1
Skylark	6	1	4	2	1	1	1	1
Ring ouzel	1	3	2	0	0	0	0	0
Short-eared owl	0	1	1	0	1	0	0	1
Pied wagtail	1	0	0	0	0	0	0	0
Wren	1	0	0	0	0	0	0	0
Mallard	0	0	1	0	0	0	0	0
Black grouse	0	0	0	0	5	0	0	0
Pheasant	0	0	0	0	0	0	0	0
Total	51	23	22	11	17	18	23	19

Table 8. Red grouse areas Pitcarmick Estate, Strath Ardle, 35, 32, 91, 74 ha.

	Dunie control			Dunie fertilised			Pitcarmick Burn *			Pitcarmick Loch		
Year	68	69	70	68	69	70	68	69	70	68	69	70
Meadow pipit	10	8	9	11	19	31	18	23	24	26	20	5
Golden plover	1	0	1	0	0	2	1	0	3	2	0	11
Curlew	1	0	3	4	0	1	5	0	0	1	0	0
Lapwing	1	0	1	6	0	0	1	0	0	0	0	0
Redshank	0	0	1	0	0	0	0	0	0	0	0	0
Snipe	0	2	0	1	0	3	0	0	1	1	0	2
Woodcock	0	0	0	0	0	0	0	0	0	0	0	0
Wheatear	0	0	0	3	0	1	0	0	0	0	0	0
Skylark	10	3	2	13	1	3	11	9	5	8	4	0
Short-eared owl	0	1	0	0	1	0	0	0	0	0	0	0
Common gull	10	0	2	0	0	0	0	0	0	0	0	0
Mallard	0	0	2	0	0	1	0	0	1	0	0	0
Black grouse	0	0	0	0	0	0	0	0	0	0	0	0
Pheasant	2	1	1	0	0	1	0	0	0	0	0	0
	35	15	22	38	21	43	36	32	34	38	24	18

* Fertilised.

Table 9. Red grouse areas Atholl Estate, 1 Glas Choire, 2 Banvie, 1a and 2a fertilised, 1b and 2b control, 114, 55, 69, 54 ha.

	1a			1b			2a			2b		
Year	68	69	70	68	69	70	68	69	70	68	69	70
Meadow pipit	25	5	15	9	14	10	18	16	15	17	18	25
Golden plover	2	11	5	2	2	2	2	0	4	3	1	3
Curlew	1	0	0	1	0	0	3	0	0	0	0	0
Lapwing	3	0	0	0	0	0	0	0	0	0	0	0
Snipe	1	2	3	1	4	1	1	0	1	0	0	1
Wheatear	0	0	0	0	0	0	0	0	0	0	0	0
Skylark	6	0	7	1	0	0	7	0	1	4	0	2
Black grouse	0	0	0	1	0	0	0	0	0	0	0	0
	38	18	30	15	20	13	31	16	21	24	19	31

Field observations over decades

Table 10. Red grouse areas in Moray, A Dallas Meikle Hill west fertilised, B Dallas east Coldburn, C Dunphail Bogeney railway fertilised, D Divie Shian a Youn control, E Moidach More west fertilised, F Moidach More east, 53, 66, 54, 58, 40, 36 ha.

Moray areas	A			B			C			D			E			F		
Year	71	72	73	71	72	73	71	72	73	71	72	73	71	72	73	71	72	73
Meadow pipit	6	5	4	8	6	4	5	5	5	6	5	5	4	5	4	4	5	4
Golden plover	3	2	2	2	2	2	2	0	0	0	0	0	1	1	0	1	0	0
Curlew	0	0	0	0	1	1	0	0	0	0	0	0	0	0	0	0	0	1
Lapwing	1	0	0	0	0	0	0	0	0	0	0	0	0	0	0	0	0	0
Snipe	0	0	1	0	1	1	1	1	0	1	1	1	2	1	0	1	0	0
Wheatear	0	0	0	0	0	0	0	1	1	0	0	0	0	0	0	0	0	0
Skylark	3	3	3	2	3	3	2	2	1	3	5	8	1	1	1	1	1	0
Mallard	0	0	0	0	0	0	0	0	0	1	2	2	0	0	0	0	0	0
Common gull	0	0	1	0	0	1	0	0	0	0	0	0	0	0	0	0	0	0
Total	13	10	11	12	13	12	10	9	7	11	13	16	8	8	5	7	6	5

Table 11. Red grouse areas on Isle of Mull, A 38, B 37, C 42, D 52 ha.

Mull	A			B			C			D		
Year	76	79	80	76	79	80	76	79	80	76	79	80
Meadow pipit	6	9	8	7	3	3	4	1	0	7	4	4
Snipe	0	0	0	2	0	0	0	0	0	0	0	0
Skylark	3	0	0	1	0	0	2	0	0	2	0	0
Golden plover	0	0	0	0	0	0	1	0	0	0	0	0
Curlew	0	0	0	0	0	0	1	0	0	0	0	0
Mallard	0	0	0	1	0	0	0	0	0	0	0	1
Wren	0	1	2	0	0	1	0	0	0	1	0	1
Total	9	10	10	11	3	4	8	1	0	10	4	6

Table 12. Ptarmigan area Meall Odhar 20 ha.

Year	64	65	66	67	68	69	70	71	96	98	2007	2008	2011
Meadow pipit	8	4	6	9	3	5	2	1	4	5	2	2	5
Golden plover	2	0	1	1	1	1	1	1	0	0	0	0	0
Wheatear	1	1	3	1	2	1	1	0	1	2	1	0	1
Dotterel	0	0	0	0	0	0	0	0	0	0	0	0	0
Ring ouzel	0	0	0	1	1	0	0	1	0	0	0	0	0
Dunlin	0	0	0	0	0	0	0	1	0	0	0	0	0
Snow bunting	0	0	0	0	0	0	0	0	0	0	0	0	0
Total	11	5	9	12	7	7	4	4	5	7	3	2	6

Table 13. Ptarmigan area on the Cairnwell, 20 ha.

Year	64	67	68	69	70	79	96	98	2004	2006	2009	2010	2011
Meadow pipit	2	7	6	2	2	2	5	2	2	2	2	3	2
Golden plover	0	0	0	0	0	0	0	0	0	0	0	0	0
Wheatear	1	1	2	1	1	2	1	1	1	1	2	2	1
Dotterel	0	0	0	0	0	0	0	0	0	0	0	0	0
Ring ouzel	0	0	0	0	0	0	0	0	0	0	0	0	0
Dunlin	0	0	0	0	0	0	0	0	0	0	0	0	0
Snow bunting	0	0	0	0	0	0	0	0	0	0	0	0	0
Total	3	8	8	3	3	4	6	3	3	3	4	5	3

Table 14. Ptarmigan study areas, A Derry Cairngorm, B Beinn a' Bhuird, C Lochnagar, D Carn nan Sac, E Cairn Lochan, F Coire Raibeirt 500, 100, 33, 70, 220, 20 ha.

	A		B	C				D		E	F
Year	61	64	70	68	69	70	71	86	87	70	86
Meadow pipit	31	29	4	3	2	10	7	5	11	4	10
Golden plover	3	2	0	2	2	2	2	0	0	1	0
Wheatear	6	5	0	1	1	0	1	8	1	1	1
Dotterel	0	0	1	1	1	0	1	0	0	6	1
Ring ouzel	1	1	0	0	0	0	0	0	0	0	0
Dunlin	0	0	0	0	0	0	0	0	0	0	0
Snow bunting	0	0	0	0	1	0	0	0	0	0	0
Total	46	37	5	7	7	9	11	13	12	12	12

Table 15. Red grouse study areas near the Cairnwell, 14, 33, 27 ha.

	Sunny Side								Loch Vrotachan		Gleann Shee top
Year	68	69	70	74	78	79	82	84	86	82	86
Meadow pipit	3	3	4	6	5	4	1	2	7	1	11
Wheatear	1	0	0	1	1	1	1	0	1	0	1
Golden plover	0	0	0	0	0	0	0	0	0	1	0
Ring ouzel	1	0	0	0	0	0	0	0	0	0	1
Total	5	3	4	7	6	5	2	2	8	2	13

Table 16. Red grouse study area on lower slopes of the Cairnwell, 13 ha.

Year	68	69	70	71	74	78	79	82	84	86	89	2006	2009	2011
Meadow pipit	5	4	2	6	5	5	5	1	2	6	5	1	1	2
Wheatear	0	0	0	0	1	0	0	0	0	1	0	0	0	0
Snipe	0	0	0	1	0	1	0	0	0	1	0	0	0	0
Total	5	4	2	7	6	6	5	1	2	8	5	1	1	2

Table 17. Red grouse areas at Kerloch i-iv 65, 75, 43, 85, v 40, vn 16, vs 16 ha.

Kerloch	i						ii		iii			iv			v	v		vn	vs
Year	61	62	63	64	71	75	62	71	62	63	65	63	64	71	62	63	64	66	66
Meadow pipit	11	2	2	8	5	12	4	4	3	1	2	10	14	13	6	1	5	6	2
Golden plover	1	2	2	2	2	2	1	1	2	3	0	2	2	3	0	0	0	0	0
Curlew	1	2	1	1	1	1	2	1	2	2	0	3	3	1	1	0	1	0	0
Lapwing	1	0	1	0	0	1	0	0	1	1	0	0	0	1	2	0	0	0	0
Snipe	3	3	1	1	1	1	0	1	1	1	0	2	3	2	0	0	0	0	2
Wheatear	3	2	3	3	2	2	3	2	2	1	0	0	1	0	0	0	0	0	0
Redshank	0	0	0	1	0	0	0	0	0	0	0	0	2	1	0	0	0	0	0
Oystercatcher	1	0	0	0	0	0	0	0	1	0	0	0	0	1	0	0	0	0	0
Skylark	4	3	2	4	3	2	1	2	2	1	0	1	4	4	2	2	1	0	0
Ring ouzel	0	1	2	1	1	1	0	0	0	0	1	0	0	0	0	0	0	0	0
Short-eared owl	0	0	1	0	0	0	0	0	0	1	0	0	0	0	0	0	0	0	0
Pied wagtail	0	1	0	0	0	0	0	0	0	0	0	0	0	0	0	0	0	0	0
Wren	0	1	0	0	0	0	0	0	0	0	0	0	0	0	0	0	0	0	0
Mallard	0	0	3	1	1	1	1	1	0	0	0	2	1	0	0	0	0	0	0
Black grouse	0	0	0	0	0	0	0	0	0	0	0	0	0	0	0	0	0	0	0
Grey partridge	0	1	0	0	0	0	0	0	2	0	1	0	0	0	0	0	0	0	0
Teal	0	1	0	0	1	0	0	0	0	0	0	0	0	0	0	0	0	0	0
Pheasant	0	0	0	0	0	0	0	0	0	0	0	0	0	0	1	0	0	0	1
Reed bunting	1	0	0	1	0	0	1	0	1	0	0	0	0	0	0	0	0	0	0
Common gull	1	0	0	0	0	2	0	0	0	0	0	10	5	7	8	4	2	1	0
Dunnock	0	0	0	0	0	0	0	0	0	0	0	0	0	0	0	0	0	1	0
Whinchat	0	0	0	0	0	0	1	0	0	0	0	0	0	0	0	0	0	0	0
Total	27	19	18	23	17	25	14	12	17	11	4	30	35	33	20	7	9	8	5

Table 18. Red grouse areas at Kerloch, vi-xiii 47, 34, 45, 28, 43, 27, 35 ha.

Kerloch	vi		vii	viii						ix		x	xi		xiii				
Year	62	67	67	65	71	73	74	75	76	65	68	71	71	75	71	74	75	76	77
Meadow pipit	12	5	5	2	15	4	7	2	2	5	3	5	10	9	2	7	7	1	1
Golden plover	0	0	2	1	1	1	1	2	1	0	0	2	0	0	1	1	1	0	0
Curlew	1	0	0	0	1	0	0	0	0	0	0	3	1	1	0	0	0	0	0
Oystercatcher	0	0	0	0	0	0	0	0	0	0	0	0	1	1	0	0	0	0	0
Snipe	0	0	0	0	0	1	0	0	0	0	0	0	1	4	0	0	0	0	0
Redshank	0	0	0	0	0	0	0	0	0	0	0	0	1	4	0	0	0	0	0
Skylark	0	0	0	0	0	0	0	0	0	0	0	0	2	3	0	0	0	0	0
Wren	0	0	0	0	0	1	0	0	0	0	0	0	0	0	0	0	0	0	0
Mallard	1	0	0	0	1	0	0	1	0	0	0	0	0	1	1	1	0	0	0
Teal	0	0	0	0	0	0	0	0	0	0	0	1	0	0	0	0	0	0	0
Pheasant	0	0	0	0	0	0	0	0	0	1	0	0	0	0	0	0	0	0	0
Pied wagtail	0	0	0	1	0	0	0	0	0	0	0	0	0	0	0	0	0	0	0
Reed bunting	0	0	0	0	0	0	1	0	0	0	0	0	0	0	0	0	0	0	0
Total	14	5	6	4	18	7	8	5	3	6	3	11	16	23	4	9	8	1	1

Table 19. Red grouse areas at Kerloch, 45, 30, 20, 11 ha.

Kerloch	xv				xvii		xix				xx
Year	74	75	76	77	74	76	71	74	75	76	77	75
Meadow pipit	15	13	7	7	7	2	2	5	4	1	1	2
Golden plover	1	1	1	1	0	0	0	0	0	0	0	0
Curlew	0	0	0	0	1	1	0	0	1	0	1	0
Wren	0	0	0	0	1	0	0	1	0	0	0	0
Mallard	0	0	0	0	0	0	0	0	0	0	0	0
Reed bunting	0	0	0	0	1	0	0	0	0	0	0	0
Pied wagtail	0	0	0	0	0	0	0	0	0	0	0	0
Total	16	14	8	8	10	3	2	6	5	1	2	2

Table 20. Red grouse study areas Elchies South and North are 1 and 2, Tilquhillie South and North are 3 and 4, 125, 125, 100, 50 ha.

	1	2	3	4
	1962	1962	1963	1963
Meadow pipit	16	24	2	1
Golden plover	1	0	1	0
Skylark	4	8	1	0
Curlew	1	1	1	0
Wheatear	0	1	0	0
Oystercatcher	0	0	1	0
Snipe	1	1	0	0
Grey partridge	1	0	0	0
Mallard	2	0	0	0
Pheasant	1	1	0	2
Pied wagtail	1	0	0	0
Short-eared owl	1	0	0	0
Common gull	0	0	15	5
Total	29	37	21	8

Table 21. Red grouse areas at Rickarton, 1 Hill of Allochie 56 ha, 2 White Hill 42 ha, 3 Round Hill 85 ha, 4 Monboy Hillocks 20 ha, 5 Bank Hill 37 ha, 6 Southwaird 27 ha, 7 W of Meikle Cross Hill 10 ha, 8 Meikle Cross Hill 66 ha, 9 E Corrie 15 ha, 10 W corrie 20 ha. 11 North slope 32 ha, 12 Curlethney Hill plateau 77ha, 13 Hill of Auquhollie 47 ha.

	1		2		3	4	5	6	7	8	9	10	11	12	13
Year	64	79	64	79	79	79	79	79	79	79	79	79	79	79	79
Meadow pipit	5	9	4	3	16	0	4	19	2	19	5	7	0	0	5
Curlew	1	1	1	1	0	0	1	1	1	1	0	0	1	0	1
Golden plover	1	0	1	0	0	0	0	0	0	0	0	0	0	0	0
Oystercatcher	0	0	0	0	0	0	0	0	0	0	0	0	1	0	0
Wheatear	0	0	0	0	0	0	0	0	0	0	0	1	0	0	0
Skylark	1	2	1	0	1	1	1	1	1	1	0	0	1	0	0
Mallard	0	0	0	0	0	0	1	0	0	0	0	0	0	0	0
Black grouse	0	0	0	0	0	0	2	0	0	1	0	0	0	0	1
Pheasant	0	0	0	0	1	0	2	1	1	1	0	1	0	0	2
Black grouse	0	0	0	0	1	0	2	0	1	0	0	0	1	0	0
Total	8	12	7	4	19	1	13	22	6	23	5	9	4	0	9

Author

Adam Watson was raised and schooled at Turriff in Aberdeenshire, close to the river Deveron, the boundary with the then Banffshire. During spring 1942 he became interested in birds, began taking notes in 1943 and daily accounts in 1944. In 1939 he became interested in the Cairngorms, and in boyhood a mountaineer and ski-mountaineer. His visits there led to the field observations on ptarmigan, red grouse, golden plover, dotterel, and other birds that form the basis of this book.

Some other books by the author

1963. Mountain hares. Sunday Times Publications, London (by AW & R. Hewson)

1970. Animal populations in relation to their food resources (Editor). Blackwell Scientific Publications, Oxford and Edinburgh

1974. The Cairngorms, their natural history and scenery. Collins, London, and 1981 Melven Press, Perth (by D. Nethersole-Thompson & AW)

1975. The Cairngorms. Scottish Mountaineering Club District Guide, published by Scottish Mountaineering Trust. Second edition published 1992

1976. Grouse management. The Game Conservancy, Fordingbridge, and the Institute of Terrestrial Ecology, Huntingdon (by AW & G.R. Miller)

1982. Animal population dynamics. Chapman and Hall, London and New York (by R. Moss, AW & J. Ollason)

1982. The future of the Cairngorms. The North East Mountain Trust, Aberdeen (by K. Curry-Lindahl, AW & D. Watson)

1984. The place names of upper Deeside. Aberdeen University Press, Aberdeen (by AW & E. Allan)

1998. The Cairngorms of Scotland. Eagle Crag, Aberdeen (by S. Rae & AW)

2008. Grouse, the grouse species of Britain and Ireland. Collins, London, New Naturalist Library No 107 (by AW & R. Moss)

2010. Cool Britannia, snowier times in 1580–1930 than since. Paragon Publishing, Rothersthorpe (by AW & I. Cameron)

2011. It's a fine day for the hill. Paragon Publishing, Rothersthorpe

2011. A zoologist on Baffin Island, 1953. Paragon Publishing, Rothersthorpe

2011. Vehicle hill tracks in northern Scotland. The North East Mountain Trust, Aberdeen, published imprint Paragon Publishing, Rothersthorpe

2011. A snow book, northern Scotland: based on the author's field observations in 1938–2011. Paragon Publishing, Rothersthorpe

2012. Some days from a hill diary: Scotland, Iceland, Norway, 1943–50. Paragon Publishing, Rothersthorpe

2012. Human impacts on the northern Cairngorms: A. Watson's scientific evidence for the 1981 Lurcher's Gully Public Inquiry into proposed Cairn Gorm ski developments, and associated papers on people and wildlife. Paragon Publishing, Rothersthorpe

2012. Birds in north-east Scotland then and now: field observations mainly in the 1940s and comparison with recent records. Paragon Publishing, Rothersthorpe (by AW & Ian Francis)

2013. Place names in much of north-east Scotland. Hill, glen, lowland, coast, sea, folk. Paragon Publishing, Rothersthorpe

2013. Points, sets and man. Pointers and setters, stars of research on grouse, ptarmigan and other game. Paragon Publishing, Rothersthorpe

www.ingramcontent.com/pod-product-compliance
Lightning Source LLC
Chambersburg PA
CBHW081257170426
43198CB00017B/2829